on track ...

The Clash

every album, every song

Nick Assirati

sonicbondpublishing.com

Sonicbond Publishing Limited

www.sonicbondpublishing.co.uk

Email: info@sonicbondpublishing.co.uk

First Published in the United Kingdom 2020

First Published in the United States 2020

British Library Cataloguing in Publication Data:

A Catalogue record for this book is available from the British Library

Copyright Nick Assirati 2020

ISBN 978-1-78952-077-4

Typeset in ITC Garamond & ITC Avant Garde

Printed and bound in England

Graphic design and typesetting: Full Moon Media

Acknowledgements

Thanks to The Clash for their music that gave me a lifetime of inspiration and strength to keep fighting. Thanks to my brothers Julian and Peter for letting me raid their Clash collections and recollections. Thanks to Indi, Dave Earl, Thad Kelly, Robert Gordon McHarg and to Huw and Lambsie for giving me the opportunity to try my hand at writing this stuff.

My sincere thanks to Steve Bell for kindly letting me reproduce his cartoons. Check out his work at www.belltoons.co.uk

Special thanks to Ali for a lifetime of love and support.

on track ...
The Clash

Contents

Preface

The intention behind this book is to make the music produced by The Clash accessible and more comprehensible to a newcomer and/or a younger audience. It is one fan's perspective [1], and an attempt to put their recorded music (particularly the lyrics) into some sort of context.

Apart from their LP records, The Clash released many singles and EPs containing songs unavailable on albums (LPs). This was part of a philosophy that fans should get value for money, so once they had bought a 7" single, there was a good chance that the A-side would not appear on any subsequent album – and if it did, then the B-side was (usually) as good as any other track on the LP. This meant that you never wasted money when buying any Clash record. When these singles, B-sides and EP tracks reappeared on later compilations, they were (at least to some extent) out of context. Songs like 'Remote Control' and 'Complete Control' only really make sense if you know the correct chronological sequence.

'Singles' and 'B-sides' may have been made to be listened to individually, but the 20-25 minute experience of listening to a vinyl LP (one side at a time) is very different to listening to a 'shuffled' digital playlist or an 80-minute CD. Songs on the triple LP set *Sandinista!* for example, may well be completely baffling to a newcomer if listened to as individual tracks. The long-playing (LP) vinyl album at its best is designed to be listened to as a complete set of songs, heard in a particular running order (albeit in two sittings) with some sort of collective coherence whereby the whole is greater than the sum of its parts. This is the reason why a 'Classic Album' can never be a 'Greatest Hits' compilation.

In this book, the albums, singles and EPs are described in chronological order so that the overall narrative is coherent. 'Academic' details like recording locations and production credits are mostly taken from sleeve notes. Further information can be found in the recommended books, on the internet or obtained by watching films like *The Clash: Westway to the World* by Don Letts.

The Clash only really made five albums, and the reason that a stinker like *Cut the Crap* emerged after this is explained if not forgiven. This album appears in the 'Not The Clash' section of the book and is followed by a selection of compilations, bootlegs, outtakes and rarities that surfaced after the band had split up. These recordings are considered to be embellishments of the chronicle rather than essential to the glorious imperfection that is the story of The Clash.

Introduction – Punk Rock and The Clash

The world is divided into two kinds of people – those who 'get' The Clash and those who don't. The Clash were a punk rock band. To understand punk rock (not the pastiche of Mohican hair, violence and aggression portrayed today) we need to go back a bit.

In the mid-1970s British society was in the doldrums. After post-World War II austerity and the collapse of empire came hope with the establishment of the Commonwealth, the National Health Service and the Welfare State. In the 1960s came The Beatles, The Rolling Stones, the civil rights movements and society gradually working towards sexual and racial equality, opening a new chapter of emancipation and personal freedom. The monolithic political blocks of the early 20th century were beginning to crumble. Britain was gradually transforming into a post-industrial society and no one really knew where we were heading. When the 1970s arrived, so did increased unemployment, high oil prices and a simmering social unrest.

Psychedelic rock and hippiedom appeared to have run their course. Music was alive and well in terms of sales, but progressive, underground and 'album-oriented rock' (AOR) seemed to be disappearing up its own arsehole. These musically complicated genres were a long way from the simple three-chord songs that anyone could play and that qualified rock and roll as truly 'The People's Music'. The alternatives were soul, disco and funk in their gentle opposition to casual and overt racism, light pop music or glam rock with its daft excess. There were notable exceptions such as the emergence of reggae, but for the (mostly) white UK working class – whose work prospects looked bleak – the cities in which they resided were in a state of general decay and the virtuoso and/or escapist music scene was disassociated from their everyday experiences. Then came The Sex Pistols.

Not quite out of nowhere – but raw rock and roll sung in the vernacular came like a shot in the arm to disaffected youth. 'GET OFF YOUR ARSE!' shouted Johnny Rotten before launching into 'Anarchy in the UK' in 1976. In a weird serendipitous moment, a spark fell on the dry tinder of UK youth and a new zeitgeist was born. The magnificent simplicity of punk rock was such that all you needed was a couple of mates, a bit of passion and something to say. The Sex Pistols kicked in the door and The Clash, The Jam, The Buzzcocks *et al* piled through. Sure there was a lot of crap tagging along too – but it did seem that for one fleeting moment the flood gates were open and a creative explosion was underway. The Do-It-Yourself attitude of punk rock empowered a generation, and over the next year spawned the 'New Wave' of music. You didn't need to be a virtuoso musician or able to play a five-minute guitar solo, as long as you had the fire in your belly and something to say. And above all, to say it like it was – both barrels blazing. Small run, locally produced punk 'fanzines' appeared all over the country, record sales reached a historical peak and interest in new music was at its zenith. In this sense, punk rock in general and The Clash, in particular, are a snapshot of British social history, but their music is so much more than a curious museum piece. All great music touches the soul, and the records made by The Clash resonate with music lovers to this day.

The Sex Pistols' *God Save The Queen* got to #1 in the UK charts during Jubilee week in 1977 despite an effective radio ban. They made one seminal album and then disappeared (despite Malcolm McLaren flogging the dead horse). Important bands like X-Ray Spex, Stiff Little Fingers and The Tom Robinson Band appeared. Pseudo-punk bands like The Police rode the bandwagon as did former pub-rockers like The Stranglers and Ian Dury. Hot on the heels of 'new wave' came the 2-Tone movement, spearheaded by The Specials and giving air time and elbow room to the likes of Madness and The Beat. UB40 were the flagship reggae band and British music was powering forward.

Paradoxically, as working class Britain began to suffer economic recession under a right-wing Thatcher government, aspirational escapism became the vogue and bands with something to say became deeply unfashionable. Fantasy became the name of the game, so the New Romantics and Electro-pop arrived, heavily influenced by the pioneering West German band, Kraftwerk. The growth of MTV and the promotional pop video became increasingly important, and style began to outweigh substance. Consequently, the UK rock and roll music scene began to decline to the extent that record sales almost halved in the early 1980s [2].

The arrival of the compact disc (CD) boosted music sales to an all time high at the turn of the century. At first, the record companies must have thought all of their Christmases had come at once. They watched the money roll in as they sold their back catalogues on CD and didn't bother investing in new artists. The joke was on them when listening to music became cheaper online and their party was over. In 2016 digital 'streaming' finally began to outstrip physical sales and downloads.

Punk rock and The Clash probably couldn't have happened in the age of the internet. There was an 'otherness' to music that they personified. The Clash were at the front line of punk. They were with The Sex Pistols on the 'Anarchy' tour of the UK in December 1976 (although few gigs actually took place on the tour due to local objections). The Clash signed to CBS in January 1977 (sparking silly cries that this was the end of punk) and recorded their eponymous first album in February that year.

Prior to The Clash, Mick Jones had been in a band called The London SS with Tony James (who went on to form Generation X with Billy Idol). After James and Jones' amicable split, Mick asked Paul Simonon to join his new band – not because he could play, but because he looked good. Mick taught Paul how to play bass and they formed a band with Keith Levene on guitar and Terry Chimes on drums and had hooked up with Bernie Rhodes [3] as their Manager. Meanwhile, John Mellor (who had metamorphosed once into 'Woody' and then into 'Joe Strummer') had been in the West London squatter scene and was playing guitar for a pub-rock band called 'The 101'ers'. He was spotted by Rhodes who suggested to Mick and Keith that they should go and see him.

They liked what they saw. Co-incidentally, the 101'ers had been supported by The Sex Pistols at a gig in April 1976 and when Joe watched The Pistols he sensed that revolution was in the air that and his old band was 'history'. Bernie arranged a meeting and Mick, Keith and Paul asked Joe to join them. Within 48 hours Joe had dumped the 101'ers and The Clash was born.

As the first punk bands were formed, the musicians reinvented themselves, often with ironic or self-deprecating stage names like Poly Styrene, Rat Scabies and Captain Sensible. John Mellor had already become Joe Strummer and gave Terry Chimes the nickname 'Tory Crimes'. Keith Levene left The Clash, soon to be followed by Chimes who liked the music but didn't like the uncompromising and fundamentalist anti-venal attitude of the members. He kindly agreed to help out and play drums for the first album before he left for good (for now). Both before and after recording their first album The Clash auditioned several drummers before settling on Nicky' Topper' Headon in April 1977. Jones had known Headon from the London SS days. Topper was more into jazz and soul, but he thought he'd join The Clash for a year 'and then move on to something good'.

It transpired that Topper was the final piece of the jigsaw. He just happened to be one of the best drummers around, so now the live performance power of The Clash started at the back, driven by Topper, then drove forward in a direct line, straight through the electrifying Strummer in the centre of the stage to hit the audience right between the eyes. Left-handed Strummer had a unique percussive power to his guitar playing – He played it right-handed which gave him great dexterity for chord shapes, but he worked his right hand like a jackhammer (hence the new surname). Mick Jones was the strutting guitar hero to his right. To his left was Paul Simonon, the epitome of The Clash, looking great with his low-slung bass and tough working class persona. Paul also brought a reggae influence with him, having been raised in Brixton, South London which had been a hotbed of West Indian music. It was usually Paul who drove the aesthetic look of the band, including the artwork for the record sleeves.

What made The Clash different was that their music had a sense of purpose and direction rooted in anti-racist street politics, articulated in Strummer's outstanding talent as a lyricist. They had decided from the beginning to do things differently. The Clash refused to appear on mainstream TV which made seeing or hearing them a labour of love in a pre-internet society – with an element of commercial suicide thrown in for good measure. The Clash would go on to release double and triple LPs for the price of a single LP and absorb the additional costs themselves through reduced royalty payments. In addition, they would generally play a series of gigs in smaller, intimate venues rather than fewer shows in larger seated venues that would have proved more lucrative for themselves. They kept ticket prices low and gained a reputation for treating their fans like human beings and were loved in return. A Clash gig was a gritty, visceral experience and always value for money.

It's true to say that The Clash never made much money while they were together from 1977-1982 and were perennially in debt to their record company, CBS. All good things come to an end and when 'Rock the Casbah' became their biggest hit to date in June 1982, Topper had just been sacked for his heroin addiction. As he sat at home, he watched The Clash on MTV (with Terry Chimes back on drums) attaining success by playing the song he had written and recorded himself. But with Topper gone, the alchemy was broken and the painful demise had begun.

Terry Chimes was back on the drum stool for the tour promoting The Clash's last album *Combat Rock*. The setlist included a lot of songs from the first LP (because they were the ones most familiar to Chimes) – and some saw this as the band's renaissance and return to core values. By now they were playing stadiums and in truth, wider commercial success somehow undermined what The Clash had always been about. They were in danger of becoming their own tribute band. What with Mick's increasing rock star prima-donna behaviour, Bernie Rhodes' attempts to steer the music (clearly out of his depth), and with Paul and Mick barely on speaking terms the inevitable came to pass. Encouraged by Bernie, Joe sacked Mick. Paul went along with it and The Clash were effectively no more. Another album *Cut the Crap* was recorded and released with some hastily recruited new members, but the album *was* crap and should never have been made, let alone released. The 'band' limped on for a while, but the writing had been on the wall for some time and Joe and Paul finally called it a day in 1986.

Apart from *Cut the Crap* (an album almost entirely disowned by Strummer), The Clash had released sixteen sides of vinyl albums, sixteen singles, five EPs (both 7" and 12") and two 12" singles in just over 5 years, the vast majority of which is of the highest quality. They toured relentlessly and worked hard. Maybe if they had taken some time off and rested, they could have stayed together for longer, but there is no guarantee that this would have been a positive outcome. They never reformed. Their legacy was boosted in hindsight and most critics would now agree that The Clash were one of the best and most important rock and roll bands of all time. As Paul later said; 'We did our job...and now we're gone and that's it. That suits me fine'.

London's Burning!

The Clash (LP – 1977)

Personnel:
Joe Strummer: vocals, guitar
Mick Jones: vocals, guitar
Paul Simonon: bass
Terry Chimes (credited as Tory Crimes): drums
Produced by Mickey Foote
UK release date: 8 April 1977
Highest position in the UK chart: 12
US release date: N/A

The Clash's first album looks and sounds like nothing else. Recorded mostly over only three weekends in February 1977, the raw energy of the band is captured by Mickey Foote's off-the-wall production. Here is something fresh, something different. Track after track of excellent songs, but the relevance of the subject matter is what really put clear water between The Clash and the vast majority of their contemporaries. CBS only allowed the band to record in a low-budget studio with Simon Humphreys whom they considered to be a 'junior' engineer, but this played right into The Clash's hands. The uncredited Humphreys did an excellent job of working out what was needed and the album was recorded with no rough edges knocked off. Joe and Mick's guitars were generally panned left and right respectively although Mick added several (by punk standards) guitar overdubs and Joe's guitar is generally low in the mix. When Joe sang his unedited vocals to the backing track, they were usually done within 2 or 3 takes. The raw feel of his singing is partly due to the fact that the vocal takes were recorded while he simultaneously played his (unplugged) guitar.

On this LP, The Clash sing about youth unemployment and disaffection, ubiquitous drug use and a brooding undercurrent of inner-city violence. Despite this, the album somehow manages to energise rather than depress. *The Clash* LP consists mostly of wonderfully pithy 2-3 minute punk rock songs and then, in the middle of Side Two comes the reggae opus 'Police & Thieves'. Its inclusion is a stroke of genius because it brings additional texture and perspective to what would otherwise be a more predictable format. It shouldn't fit into the album, but it absolutely does and keeps the door open for a whole new musical direction which the band were to explore more fully as time went on. This is Mick Jones' favourite Clash album, most of the songs having been written prior to going into the recording studio.

The Clash had been unable to locate a permanent drummer at that point, so although Terry Chimes played drums for the LP, he does not feature on the artwork. The front cover shows the three permanent members of the band looking tough in a Camden Town alleyway (so far so usual), but the rear of the sleeve shows a police charge under The Westway at the Notting Hill

Carnival from the previous year. Immediately the impression given is that this band has something to say – and they did. The basic colours, the high contrast images and simple text typeface echo the look of a contemporary, low-budget fanzine, emphasising the DIY punk ethic. The Clash's first album was an instant classic and sold well in the UK, however, it was not released in the USA for another two years (and even then with content that had been heavily edited). The Clash had raised the bar for punk. There have been many imitators, but this album stands head and shoulders above the rest. The quality of the songwriting, the freshness of the performance and the groundbreaking nature of the band themselves make this album indispensable. If you don't have this LP, then get it.

Side One
'Janie Jones' (Strummer/Jones) Lead vocal – Joe
Written by Mick Jones on the number 31 bus on the way to rehearsal at Camden Town, and named after a well known singer and brothel keeper of the time [4], 'Janie Jones' begins with a double chorus declaring the subject matter – sex, drugs and rock and roll. Mick knew what he wanted and instructed Terry Chimes on how to play the now iconic drum intro. The monotone melody and bass guitar in the chorus reflect the monotony of the daily grind to the working man. In early live recordings Mick can be heard singing the lyric in the first person i.e.

I'm in love with Rock and roll / I'm in love with getting stoned
I'm in love with Janie Jones / I don't like my boring job, no!

Joe knocked the lyric about which shifted the subject matter to the third person – an archetypal frustrated young man, who hates his job and his boss:

But it seems like everyone, he's got a Ford Cortina
That just won't run without fuel.

The track also contains a huge dose of humour, something which was evident all throughout The Clash's canon, although widely ignored by the press who labelled Strummer' Po-faced Joe'. In the first verse, Strummer throws in 'You lucky lady' to the girl of our hero, while 'Fill her up, Jacko!' thrown in at the end of the second verse, has been repeated many times by a Clash fan in the petrol station.

'Janie Jones' is a basic three-chord song on E, A and B, and with the lyric now updated becomes the opening salvo of this most iconic of punk albums. The simple but effective instrumentation and raw production capture the energy of the moment perfectly.

This is the opening shot from 'The only band that matters'. The Clash considered releasing it as a single, but events overtook them when the record company put out 'Remote Control' instead.

'Remote Control' (Strummer/Jones) Lead vocal – Mick / Joe

With this track, the lead vocal is shared between Mick and Joe and the whole song is more nuanced in construction than most Clash songs of the period. It starts with a fairly standard thumping punk intro but then includes the C major to B bass that gives the melancholy feel to the start of each verse, bookended with the D/Dsus4 lick at the end. This is an early indication of Mick's interest in moving forward from three-chord punk thrashes (prompting Joe to describe it as a 'mini-opera'), although it still includes a gloriously simple guitar solo by Mick.

In the UK, pubs closed at 11pm in the 1970s and the song expresses the boredom and frustration of living in a state of dull monochrome conformity and articulates a sense of disempowerment:

It's so grey in London town, Panda car crawling around
Here it comes, 11 o'clock – Where can we go now?

A panda car was a police vehicle. The 'meeting in Mayfair' refers to a meeting of record company executives in an expensive London area wherein the decision was made to withdraw support from the band's tour with The Sex Pistols. The song goes on to question authority 'Look out for rules and regulations' and criticises politicians in Parliament as being '...fat and old / Queuing for the House of Lords...'

Joe takes over the lead vocal at the end refrain by counterpointing with Mick. The phrase 'I obey' was used by Daleks – a type of wicked automaton from the then-popular BBC science fiction television series *Doctor Who*.

'I'm So Bored With The USA' (Strummer/Jones) Lead vocal – Joe

When Joe and Mick sat down to write songs together, Mick had a song 'I'm so bored with you-u-u' which Joe changed to 'I'm so bored with the U-S-A' and then rewrote the verses. The intro has echoes of 'Pretty Vacant' by The Sex Pistols – hard to know who was ripped off by whom.

Mick's lead guitar plays the intro and gives the melodic counterbalance to the vocal. Joe plays his 'choppy' guitar style while the bass stays more or less on the root note.

Lyrically, Joe juxtaposes the projected veneer of righteous American TV cops ('Starsky' and 'Kojak') with the grimy underbelly of US gun violence, the Watergate scandal and Vietnam veterans hooked on heroin.

Yankee soldier, he wanna shoot some skag
He met it in Cambodia but now he can't afford a bag.

The song is a cry against the creeping Americanisation of world culture and not against the American people themselves about whom Joe was always complementary.

'White Riot' (Strummer/Jones) Lead vocal – Joe

Non-stop momentum from the '1-2-3-4' count in from Mick to the end, less than two minutes away. Strummer and Simonon were infamously present at the 1976 Notting Hill Carnival when it metamorphosed into a riot with running battles between black youths and the police. In the lyric, Strummer wants to know, if black people are OK to stick it to the authorities by rioting, then why aren't white people doing the same? 'Everybody's doing just what they're told to'.

'White Riot' is a call to arms – stop taking this shit, get some balls like your black neighbours and do something about it. The version of the song included on the LP had actually already been recorded as a demo in an 8-track studio in Beaconsfield a few months earlier. This 'Beaconsfield' version which was remixed by Simon Humphrey for inclusion on the album has one of Joe's trademark ad-libs instead of a third verse.

'Hate And War' (Strummer/Jones) Lead vocal – Mick

Love and Peace was seen in the punk era as a hippy thing and so not particularly relevant. The Clash enjoyed turning the 1960s mantra on its head to express the new perceived reality: 'Hate and War / The only things we've got today'. Mick goes eye to eye with the hostile monster of snidey violence dished out to anyone seen as being different: 'If I get aggression / I'll give it two times back'. (The theme of being attacked in the street just for being yourself was revisited in 'The City of the Dead'). The lyric attacks all bigotry and the music is structured with an offbeat guitar in the verses and punctuated with a thumping emphasis at the intro and chorus. The lead guitar alternates with the vocal in a 'question and answer' style during the verses. The attention-grabbing title 'Hate and War' focuses the listener's attention and Mick's vocal performance has an element of desperation to it – He means it, man!

'What's My Name' (Strummer/Jones/Levene) Lead vocal – Joe

From the opening guitar riff that gives a sense of foreboding, through the rumbling floor-tom drum beats in the four-line verses, this is classic punk. The hook on the chorus is half shouted/half sung over Paul's rising bassline and Mick's whining guitar. 'What the hell is wrong with me?' This is a great track, exploring the mental state of a teenager from a dysfunctional home – 'Dad got pissed, so I got clocked' (i.e. Dad got drunk, so I got punched), trying to orientate himself in a confusing world. He deals with his loneliness and low self-esteem with violence, gets in trouble with the law and ends up as a sociopath breaking into people's homes. The loose lyrical element of 'What's my name' was a perfect platform for Joe to al-lib and to alter the words when played live (There is superb footage of the band performing this tune at the Belle Vue in Manchester on 15 November 1977). The song was co-written with Keith Levene who was in the embryonic band with Mick and Paul before Joe joined. Keith later stated that it was he who came up with the ascending note sequence under the chorus. He was part of the original line-up, but left before the first album was recorded and went on to play guitar in Public Image Limited (PiL) with John Lydon (aka Johnny Rotten) after the Sex Pistols had split up.

'Deny' (Strummer/Jones) Lead vocal – Joe

'Deny' has a slightly un-punk aspect to it, beginning with a fade-in and containing an outro refrain that not only lasts for a third of the entire song, but also ends with an un-punk fade-out. Chrissie Hynde (later of The Pretenders) is acknowledged by Joe to have had some input into the extended outro – a feature that gives Joe a chance to perform another of his trademark vocal ad-libs.

This was one of the first Clash songs to be performed live and has shades of The Pistols' 'Liar' (although again it is uncertain who copied whom). The song mentions '…going out to The 100 Club' which was an early punk venue in Oxford Street. This is The Clash's first anti-heroin song and has Strummer pointing out that this particular junkie can't be trusted 'You wouldn't know the truth if it hit you in the eye'. Being a true friend, Joe points out that 'You said you ain't had none for weeks / But Baby, I've seen your arms'. 'Deny' can be seen as the start of a continuum running through 'Drug-stabbing Time', 'Hateful' and on through to 'Ghetto Defendant' – against the debilitating consequences of using hard drugs.

'London's Burning' (Strummer/Jones) Lead vocal – Joe

This is one of The Clash's finest early songs. Joe remembered having to write the song down quietly because, at the moment of his inspiration, his girlfriend (Palmolive, of The Slits) was in bed asleep. 'London's Burning' has all the hallmarks of one of Joe's from the rhythmic percussive chords, through the punchy feel of the music expressing a pent-up frustration with the status quo. 'London's Burning' is the name of a children's nursery song/round which harks back to the Great Fire of London in 1666. When Joe and Mick started writing together, Mick was living with his Gran in her 18th floor flat in Wilmcote House in the Warwick Estate just off Harrow Road. This flat with its panoramic view across the city also overlooked The Westway (which is an elevated section of the A40 trunk road out of West London). The sense of disenchantment experienced by looking across a city sedated by TV is articulated

> Black or white you turn it on, you face the new religion
> Everybody's sitting 'round watching television

as is the use of Speed (Amphetamine Sulphate) – this being the recreational drug of choice in punk circles at the time. Joe uses the fast-flowing traffic on the Westway to make the point with the pun; 'I can't think of a better way to spend the night / Than speeding around underneath the yellow lights'. In contrast to the verses, the chorus has a punching rhythm underpinning the lyric 'London's burning with boredom now / London's burning, dial 9-9-9-9-9' as the narrator frantically and comically over-dials '999' in his desperate attempt to call the fire brigade so that they can put out the metaphorical flames (Joe was incidentally later to support the Fire Brigade Union in their struggle to achieve fair pay in 2002). The final verse has a rather poetic Strummer lost in an inner-city housing estate while 'The wind howls through the empty blocks looking for a home'. This song ends Side One with Joe's voice echoing in the listener's ears 'London's burning!'

Side Two
'Career Opportunities' (Strummer/Jones) Lead vocal – Joe
The Clash's manager, Bernie Rhodes, encouraged the band to write about issues that affected their own lives. Paul was thumbing through the jobs section of a local newspaper when he suggested the title of this song. Subject matter did not come any more relevant to young people than this. Joe wrote the lyrics and presented them to Mick who came up with the tune. This simple method became the template for the Strummer/Jones songwriting team that was the backbone of The Clash. Paul was often involved as a final 'filter' for this creative partnership, for example, he later recounted how he refused to allow a lyric about pensions into this song.

Opportunity Knocks was a contemporary British TV talent show in 1977. The fact that in this song, Joe describes 'Career Opportunities' as being 'The one that never knocks' pins a gallows-humour onto the rising levels of youth unemployment at the time. The absence of any prospect of a fulfilling occupation and the subsequent life sentence of grinding monotony is rightly challenged here. Joe states his opposition to becoming cannon-fodder 'I hate the army and I hate the RAF / I don't want to go fighting in the tropical heat' and simultaneously points out that dead-end jobs are only ever offered as an alternative to law-breaking and prison 'any job they offer you is to keep you out (of) the dock'. The inability to get a decent job is a perennial problem for young adults from working class communities and so this song expresses the real life experience of young people from non-privileged backgrounds.

'Cheat' (Strummer/Jones) Lead vocal – Joe
'Cheat' starts with a great lyric 'I get violent when I'm fucked up / I get silent when I'm drugged up' but is arguably the weakest track on the LP. The song takes the nihilism of violence and drug use as a starting point and then follows these themes through to their natural destiny of aggressive dishonesty. The lyric can be viewed as an ironic rejection of the 'Greed is good' capitalist system that views selfishness and deceit as virtuous. If the only way to achieve success in such a system is to lie and to cheat your way to the top, then the system itself has to be questioned. Musically 'Cheat' is typical punk song with thumping chords emphasising the lyrics. There is also a heavy phasing effect used during the track which keeps the overall sound more interesting up to the somewhat un-punk 'fade-out'.

'Protex Blue' (Strummer/Jones) Lead vocal – Mick
Mick had been listening to The Ramones' first album and the influence is evident in this thrash-punk classic. The opening syncopated guitar lick gives a sense of urgency and when the band kicks in, he takes the lead vocal. Looking for love, he buys some 'Protex' condoms from a machine in a toilet

– 'The bog of a West End Bar'. After a frustrating and unfulfilling evening, the singer sits in a train on the London Underground Bakerloo line, trying to get home. Desperate for a girlfriend and bombarded with pornography through 'erotica' and 'skin flicks' – and maybe after using a prostitute – the singer ends up shouting 'Johnny, Johnny!' (slang for a condom). Ultimately dissatisfied, seduced by advertisements, unable to get the girl, this is one minute forty-seven seconds of one young man's sexual, emotional and moral exasperation. Written by Mick prior to Joe joining the band.

'Police & Thieves' (Murvin/Perry) Lead vocal – Joe

When punk first started there were very few punk records for the DJs like Don Letts to play at the clubs, so he played reggae and dub which resulted in many punk rockers tuning in to those genres from the off. Paul Simonon grew up in Brixton and was particularly keen to bring a reggae influence to the band. Originally written by Jamaican singer Junior Murvin and Lee Perry, and performed in falsetto by Murvin, the sentiment of 'Police & Thieves' is one of antipathy towards violence from the point of view of an innocent bystander caught in the crossfire.

Junior Murvin's original 'Police and Thieves' became well known in the summer of 1976 and was especially relevant in the Notting Hill Carnival of that year. The Clash used to play around with this song in rehearsals and decided to try and record a version for the album. This was mildly controversial at the time because it was a clear departure from the three-chord thrash that was the bread and butter of contemporary punk. Mick's arrangement with his and Joe's guitars complementing each other and panned to opposite speakers is unmistakable. After a short introduction, the music sits in a 'punk/white' reggae arrangement which misses out the usual percussive emphasis on the third beat of the bar. The track is also significantly longer than any other on the album and includes a Strummer ad-lib towards the end.

The inclusion of a 'punk reggae' track on the album did more than just open doors for The Clash's future musical direction; it also made a political statement. Punk rock was essentially the music of the white working class and punk bands made a point of singing in their own accents and referencing their own locality in terms of culture, people and places – for example, Paul sports a Union 'Jack' flag on the front cover of *The Clash* album cover. Alongside this assertion of identity and much more worryingly, some early punks had been trying to be 'provocative' by ignorantly flirting with Nazi kitsch including swastikas. This potentially opened the door for the far-right politicisation of punk, which was later to culminate in the 'Oi!' subgenre which was (almost totally) hijacked by racist politicians.

The Clash were anti-racist from the start and could sense that songs like 'White Riot' might be misinterpreted. They were having none of it, and although they were at pains to explain this to journalists, the inclusion of 'Police & Thieves' on their album made the point better than a thousand interviews. It drew a line in the sand. It opened the eyes and ears of fans to a punk version of a quintessentially black music genre. It was a musical and political masterstroke.

'48 Hours' (Strummer/Jones) Lead vocal – Joe

Written quickly at Clash HQ (Rehearsal Rehearsals), this song about only being able to enjoy life at the weekend has Joe taking 'the Tube' (which is the name of the London Underground railway) to town in a frantic attempt to get his thrills because:

> Monday's coming like a jail on wheels.

In the same vein as 'Protex Blue', the singer has under two minutes to express his frustration at failing to find a girlfriend 'You know a girl, yeah – well, she's bound to be rude' and not getting the satisfaction he needs before the weekend is over. Glancing back to 'Janie Jones', the singer is in a job he hates and misses his kicks because he 'ain't got a ticket'.

'Garageland' (Strummer/Jones) Lead vocal – Joe

When The Clash played in Islington, London in August 1976 the music critic Charles Shaar Murray described them as 'the kind of garage band who should be speedily returned to the garage, preferably with the engine running'[5]. The Clash retort was to state clearly that they were happy to stay in 'Garageland' and away from seeking the approval of any of the music critics. Joe's 'bullshit detector' meant that the band intended to steer a new course between 'contracts', 'new boots' and being asked to 'wear suits' (see 'All The Young Punks' from the second LP). 'Garageland' is only a little longer than the other original songs on this album and yet it seems to have an epic feel and is a perfect closing track. Mick's wistful backing vocals in the chorus add an element of pathos to the defiant determination that underpins the theme.

Putting up with the air pollution in the unwanted spaces used for band rehearsals was part of the deal, and the band revel in the contrast of their humble surroundings and the detached lifestyles of the privileged few.

> I don't want to hear about what the rich are doing
> I don't want to go to where the rich are going.

The Clash set themselves up in opposition to the existing state of affairs despite the lack of equipment '22 singers – One microphone' and an uphill struggle, they intend to stay true to their principles. Similar declarations were made by many, but very few bands left a legacy as intact as that of The Clash.

'White Riot' (7" Single – 1977)

Personnel:
Joe Strummer: vocals, guitar

Mick Jones: vocals, guitar
Paul Simonon: bass
Terry Chimes: drums
Produced by Mickey Foote
UK release date: 18 March 1977.
Highest chart position in the UK: 38
US release date: N/A

A-side
'White Riot' (single version) (Strummer/Jones) Lead vocal – Joe

> White riot, I wanna riot. White riot – a riot of my own.

Released three weeks before The Clash's first album, 'White Riot' is the epitome of a punk single at just under two minutes long – Get in, say what you want to say and then get off – and with no cheesy fade-outs. Start with a bang and finish with a bang. This version is slightly longer than the one on the LP. Listen out for the old-style police siren at the beginning and the alarm bell at the end. Recorded in the same sessions as the first LP, this version also contains a third verse with the lines;

> Are you taking over or are you taking orders?
> Are you going backwards or are you going forwards?

The idea of the do-it-yourself empowerment that punk rock unleashed is evident in the simple 'anyone can do this' structure of the music, but is also illustrated on the front sleeve wherein the band had fashioned their own aesthetic by writing song titles and lyrics on their clothes, often using stencils. Simonon and Rhodes gave particular attention to the artwork for the records and the overall 'look' of the band. 'White Riot' was released in a picture sleeve (a feature in itself which at that time was synonymous with 'punk') and with Chimes having already left the band, it only showed Jones, Strummer and Simonon on the front (as on the first LP, although this time in a pose not dissimilar to the LP cover of *State of Emergency* by Joe Gibbs and the Professionals).

B-side
'1977' (Strummer/Jones) Lead vocal – Joe

At an even shorter 1 minute 41 seconds, the B-side '1977' continues the 'Year-Zero' [6] approach harnessed by punk bands (at least for the time being) that everything prior to 1977 was irrelevant, hence 'No Elvis, Beatles or The Rolling Stones'. Joe was hesitant about using this line from his notebook, but Mick liked it and into the lyric it went. (The irony is that the chords sound like they've been lifted from a Kinks record). The song contains a warning to the rich residing in exclusive London neighbourhoods like Knightsbridge that things were about to change.

The UK was ostensibly celebrating Queen Elizabeth II's silver jubilee in 1977, and the song ends with a countdown from 1977 and on through to 1984 – referencing the novel of the same name by George Orwell.

'Capital Radio EP' (7" EP – 1977)
Personnel:
Joe Strummer: vocals, guitar
Mick Jones: vocals, guitar
Paul Simonon: bass
Terry Chimes: drums
Produced by Mickey Foote
UK release date: 9 April 1977.
Highest chart position in the UK: N/A
US release date: N/A

The *Capital Radio EP* is extremely rare. It was not officially 'released', but was given away to fans that sent off a sticker issued with the first 10,000 copies of their debut album along with a coupon from the *New Musical Express (NME)* which was an important weekly music paper of the day (and was generally supportive of the punk rock movement). The photograph on the rear of the picture sleeve initially showed Joe's graffiti of the words 'White Riot' on the windows of the reception area of the Capital Radio offices in London, but was 'withdrawn' when Bernie Rhodes decided that this was too provocative, even for The Clash.

Side One
'Listen' (Strummer/Jones) / Interview
The first track on Side One ('Listen') is a short instrumental introduction that spills into the following track which is an interview of the band with Tony Parsons of the NME, poorly recorded on a London Underground train on 21 March 1977. 'Listen' was performed at very early Clash gigs but was dropped when other tunes were written to replace it. In interview Joe recounted how Paul (being a novice on the bass guitar) was so nervous that when they played this tune at the first gig that he lost his composure and mistakenly continued the rising bass line in the introduction to such an extent that the band couldn't play the song at all, and they all fell about laughing. The full version of 'Listen' is available on the *Super Black Market Clash* compilation. When released as part of the *Sound System* reissue, the interview was edited. The opening track on Side Two is a continuation of the interview; however the real treasure on the record is the second track on Side Two – 'Capital Radio'.

Side Two
'Interview' / 'Capital Radio' (Strummer/Jones) Lead vocal – Joe
Capital Radio was and is an independent commercial radio station in London. It was set up to provide an alternative to the BBC and thereby replace the

hitherto unlicensed 'pirate' radio stations. These had been transmitting from boats positioned offshore in order to avoid UK government control and regulation. Almost all UK pirate radio stations were shut down in the 1960s and Capital Radio was set up to replace them in the London area. The choice of music played on the air was effectively controlled by the Director of Programmes – Aiden Day (name-checked in the song). The jingle went 'Capital radio – in tune with London' – a point on which The Clash took a different view, referring to the station output as 'The Dr Goebbels Show', thereby comparing it to Nazi propaganda – perhaps a bit harsh. The lyric also attacks the voyeuristic nature of some of the programmes wherein members of the public were encouraged to phone in to disclose their emotional and relationship problems.

The track opens with drums, Staccato guitar and bass, then a simple verse/bridge/verse/bridge construction, including another piss-take of a Capital Radio jingle '...all the hits...' and with no chorus as such until the outro when Jonesy repeats the mantra of 'Capital Radio', for Joe to counterpoint 'In tune with nothing' building up to his magnificent ad-lib vocal finale, culminating in 'Don't touch that dial!'

Recorded on the 3 April 1977 along with 'Listen', 'Capital Radio' was the last studio recording to feature Terry Chimes and is early Clash at their best. There is an excellent live version of the song on the *From Here To Eternity* album. The original version of the song later reappeared on the *Black Market Clash* compilation mini-LP as 'Capital Radio One' (to distinguish it from the version of the same song that appeared in 1979 on *The Cost Of Living EP*).

'Remote Control' (7" Single – 1977)
Personnel:
Joe Strummer: vocals, guitar
Mick Jones: vocals, guitar
Paul Simonon: bass
Terry Chimes: drums
Produced by Mickey Foote / The Clash
UK release date: 13 May 1977.
Highest chart position in the UK: 51
US release date: N/A

A-side
'Remote Control' (Strummer/Jones) Lead vocal – Mick/Joe
Identical to album version (above). 'Remote Control' was released as a single by the record company without the band's permission.

B-side
'London's Burning' (live) (Strummer/Jones) Lead vocal – Joe
This live version was taken from the *White Riot Promo* film recorded in April 1977 (available on the *Sound System* compilation), except that this version has

been edited from the original film performance to swap the first and second verses around. The recording gives some insight into the power and energy of an early live performance by the band, but misses out the classic Strummer ad-lib at the end as on the LP version. The front of the sleeve is a monochrome copy of the album cover with red highlights and a similar punk 'look' to the sleeve for 'White Riot', however, the text on the back reads like thinly veiled record company hype. It is clear that The Clash had nothing to do with the release other than encouraging their fans not to buy it.

'Complete Control' (7" Single – 1977)

Personnel:
Joe Strummer: vocals, guitar
Mick Jones: vocals, guitar
Paul Simonon: bass
Topper Headon: drums
Gary Barnacle: saxophone
Steve Nieve: keyboards
Produced by Lee 'Scratch' Perry [7] / Mickey Foote
UK release date: 23 September 1977.
Highest chart position in the UK: 28
US release date: N/A

A-side
'Complete Control' (Strummer/Jones) Lead vocal – Joe
As good a drummer as Terry Chimes might have been; the band became truly complete with the addition of Nicky 'Topper' Headon. The introduction to 'Complete Control' has a harder and sharper feel with Topper driving the momentum with incisive bass drum beats alongside the great opening guitar riff. Recorded in August 1977, this is the first release from The Clash with the classic band line-up and the performance is on a corresponding higher level. Power and energy burst out of the speakers – These gentlemen are severely pissed off and they're about to tell you why.

They said 'release Remote Control' / But we didn't want it on the label.

CBS released 'Remote Control' as a single without consulting The Clash. Then Bernie Rhodes had made the band laugh by insisting that he wanted 'complete control' over The Clash. Mick Jones came back the next day with this song, part piss-take of Bernie, but mostly an attack on CBS. Mick's incendiary guitar playing is ironically praised by Joe after the solo as he calls out 'You're my guitar hero!' One of the many reasons that The Clash were exceptional was the fact that they didn't behave like aloof 'Stars', but instead tried very hard to treat their fans like human beings. While the mainstream British newspapers were busy attacking punk rock fans as 'filth', The Clash were becoming renowned for letting the same people in for free through the back doors of venues they were playing at. At that time the punk bands were not only getting hassle from record companies and the authorities, but punks, in general, were also in danger of getting attacked in the streets (a theme addressed in the B-side 'City of the Dead'). In the outro, the backing vocals point out that the whole situation is a 'C-O-N' to which we are all subject – 'That means you!'

B-side
'City Of The Dead' (Strummer/Jones) Lead vocal – Joe
The general air of hostility to punk rock and towards the people that listened to it was stoked and encouraged by the media. The disappointing and inevitable consequence of this was that punk rockers were becoming frequent victims of unprovoked attacks by thugs in the streets. Joe and Mick looked out across a city pacified, sedated and stifled by violence, apathy and television. The song opens with a saxophone solo played by Gary Barnacle, a friend of Topper which helps to give the song an upbeat feel despite the sadness expressed in the lyrics. 'New York Johnny' is a reference to ex-New York Doll, Johnny Thunders who supported The Clash on the 'Anarchy' tour with his new band, The Heartbreakers.

The Sci-Fi title and melancholy lyric paint a picture of social dystopia, but the song is one of defiance rather than despair and punks were encouraged to hold the line against the jerks:

What we wear is dangerous gear / It'll get you picked up anywhere
Though we get beat up we don't care / At least it livens up the air.

Some critics attacked this record as an indication that The Clash had somehow lost direction, but the opposite is actually true. Musically it was a move towards higher quality performance and a more imaginative arrangement, while the lyrics are reflective but positive. The Clash perspective on punk rock was about empowerment and a new perspective.

'Clash City Rockers' (7" Single – 1978)
Personnel:
Joe Strummer: vocals, guitar, piano
Mick Jones: vocals, guitar
Paul Simonon: bass
Topper Headon: drums
Produced by Mickey Foote
UK release date: 17 February 1978.
Highest chart position in the UK: 35
US release date: N/A

A-side
'Clash City Rockers' (Strummer/Jones) Lead vocal – Joe
Recorded at CBS between September and November 1977, and beginning with

a riff ripped off from 'I Can't Explain' by The Who, 'Clash City Rockers' is a well-performed record with a partly self-promoting lyric, but more importantly, a call to arms. The 'Rockers' referred to in the title of the song may be a sub-genre of reggae, but The Clash began in earnest to create their own myth with this classic rock tune. They are broadcasting a sort of 'Piss or get off the pot' attitude and looking to create a culture of fraternal solidarity and a bunker mentality for the besieged Clash faithful – 'Quit your dead-end job and join the revolution' sort of thing.

> ...Then you realise that you got to have a purpose
> Or this place is gonna knock you out sooner or later.

The lyric also includes a parody of the children's nursery rhyme 'Oranges and lemons' therein taking more pot-shots at the Rock establishment.

After the direct, off-the-wall street sound of the first album and the follow-up single 'Complete Control' which cover the subject matter of disenfranchised youth via life in inner-city estates, drug use, boredom and unemployment, The Clash are looking for the next step. The Sex Pistols finish their first record, ('Anarchy In The UK') with Johnny Rotten shouting 'Get pissed, D-E-S-T-R-O-Y!' the logic of which appears to be to tear down the stale status quo so that something new can happen. At the same time, Paul Weller and The Jam are looking for the energy and artistic freedom of punk to lead to a new wave of young artists, poets and musicians who can bring about something better. In the single 'All Around The World' Weller sings 'What's the point in saying "Destroy"? / We want a new life for everywhere'.

So as punk rock metamorphosed into a beast with several different heads, The Sex Pistols cornered the market of nihilism, The Damned took on the role of slapstick clowns, The Jam promoted a youth explosion of creativity, and The Clash were gradually moving towards becoming the standard-bearers of a new form of visceral street politics...with guitars.

When Bernie Rhodes heard this recording, he described it as 'a bit flat' and so, on his orders Mickey Foote sped it up, thereby increasing the pitch by around a semitone. This speeded up version was released as the single without the band's knowledge or permission and they were furious. Foote was sacked and most subsequent re-releases of the song have been the original version at the correct pitch and tempo.

B-side
'Jail Guitar Doors' (Strummer/Jones) Lead vocal – Mick
Recorded in September 1977, 'Jail Guitar Doors' was born when Mick recycled the chorus of one of Joe's songs from 'The 101'ers'. He changed the words in the verses to produce a new version about the previous rock 'n' roll heroes that had fallen foul of drugs. The song name-checks 'Wayne' (Kramer of MC5), 'Pete' (Green of Fleetwood Mac [8]) and 'Keith' (Richards of The Rolling Stones). A lyric that eulogises and shows deference towards 'established' Rock

The Clash ... *On Track*

Stars was clearly at odds with The Clash's 'year-zero' stance towards their predecessors. In addition, the implied ambivalence towards hard drug use in general and drug-induced self-mutilation, in particular, reveals a philosophical inconsistency with songs like 'Deny' and 'London's Burning'.

'Jail Guitar Doors' is a well-performed punk/pop song that exposes a slight lack of focus about what The Clash were trying to do and what they stood for. But that was all about to change with the next single…

'(White Man) In Hammersmith Palais' (7" Single – 1978)

Personnel:
Joe Strummer: vocals, guitar, piano
Mick Jones: vocals, guitar, harmonica
Paul Simonon: bass
Topper Headon: drums
Produced by The Clash
UK release date: 16 June 1978.
Highest chart position in the UK: 32
US release date: N/A

A-side
'(White Man) In Hammersmith Palais' (Strummer/Jones) Lead vocal – Joe

The Clash were on the road to becoming a truly great band with this, their self-produced fifth single. The Hammersmith Palais was a West London dance venue with a sprung dance floor, and Don Letts took Joe to a Jamaican reggae event there on 5 June 1977. The artists name checked in the first verse; Dillinger, Leroy Smart and Delroy Wilson, were on the bill. Strummer was expecting some sort of radical black experience and was somewhat disappointed to find that tired of all the bullshit they had to endure in their day jobs; the black community simply wanted to dress nicely and go dancing on their evenings out.

Joe wrote the lyrics, gave them to Mick and classic was born. Musically, the track is breaking new ground for the band as they push back their own boundaries and come up with an original 'white reggae' arrangement. Simonon is well and truly at home driving the bassline, whilst Topper plays with a broken hi-hat pedal giving an off-centre twist to the razor-sharp percussion. This is also where The Clash began to nail their collective colours to the mast as anti-fascists. At that time the neo-Nazi 'National Front' was starting to attract support from the disaffected and disenfranchised white working class of Britain. Whilst loosely on the socialist left, The Clash never claimed to know all the answers. However, they were staunchly anti-racist (not at all common at the time).

White youth, Black youth – Better find another solution
Why not phone up Robin Hood and ask him for some wealth distribution?

25

Some of the more politically naïve elements of the punk movement were sporting swastikas. Others were flirting with violence, hedonism and mindless destruction – and Strummer could smell the far-right potentially cashing in:

> If Adolf Hitler flew in today they'd send a limousine anyway

The Clash mindset was beginning to crystallise around the street politics of unity and social justice, whilst trying to remain unsullied by resisting the allure of a Faustian pact with the music industry. With an over the shoulder glance back to 'Garageland', Strummer asks 'You think it's funny, turning rebellion into money?' With the magnificent '(White man) In Hammersmith Palais', The Clash had put themselves head and shoulders above the vast majority of their contemporaries.

This single was the first by The Clash not to have a picture sleeve, but was issued with four different colour 'classic-style' sleeves – blue, green, yellow and pink. The A-side of the label had the image of a revolver and the B-side was the image of a victim being shot – '...it won't get you anywhere fooling with guns'.

The original single version was recorded at CBS studios in February 1978 (just before Joe was hospitalised with hepatitis) and then finished off at the Marquee sessions a few weeks later. Another studio version produced by Sandy Pearlman with slightly different lyrics was recorded in Basing Street Studios in May 1978 and was subsequently donated to the *Rock Against Racism* LP that was released in 1980.

B-side
'The Prisoner' (Strummer/Jones) Lead vocal – Mick
'The Prisoner' (named after a 1960s UK cult-fantasy TV show) is a straight forward punk-pop song with the main author, Mick Jones on lead vocal. It name-checks a few London locations and points to an escape from boredom through music. It was recorded in March 1978 at Marquee Studios in Soho, London. The lyric refers to adolescent frustration with suburban decency and compliance and appears to be at least to some extent autobiographical. The song mentions 'Johnny Too Bad' by The Slickers and 'Johnny B. Goode' by Chuck Berry, pointing to the rock/reggae crossover that The Clash were championing at the time – a banner enthusiastically picked up by others including Sting in songs such as 'Roxanne' and 'The Bed's Too Big Without You'.

When Joe and Paul were arrested after a gig at The Glasgow Apollo in 1978, a fan started singing 'The Prisoner' to them while they were in the police cells. The song became emotionally important to the band thereafter, consequently finding its way into several live shows over the following years.

What Are We Supposed To Do?

Give 'em Enough Rope (LP – 1978)

Personnel:
Joe Strummer: vocals, guitar, piano
Mick Jones: vocals, guitars, piano
Paul Simonon: bass, backing vocals
Topper Headon: drums
Allen Lanier: piano (uncredited)
Stan Bronstein: saxophone (uncredited)
Bob Andrews: keyboards (uncredited)
Produced by Sandy Pearlman
UK release date: 10 November 1978.
Highest position in the UK chart: 2
US release date: 17 November 1978.
Highest chart position in the US: 128

After establishing themselves with their first album and a string of great singles, The Clash found themselves where most bands find themselves at that point in their musical careers – with the record company now asking about a second album. The band had written almost all of the original songs for the first album prior to recording it and what with the release of the three subsequent 'stand-alone' singles; they didn't actually have much material for a new LP. As a consequence, at the end of 1977, Bernie Rhodes sent Joe and Mick to Jamaica to get some inspiration. They wandered around Kingston for a while and then came up with 'Drug-Stabbing Time' and 'Safe European Home' relatively quickly. Once back in London, Mick, Joe and Topper recorded some basic 4-track demos so that Paul could learn the basslines.

Rhodes had selected Sandy Pearlman from a list of producers presented to him by CBS for the next record. Pearlman was already established as an album-oriented-rock (AOR) producer in the US and was seen by record company executives as a safe pair of hands to make a Clash album that would be more palatable for a US audience. There was an inauspicious start to the relationship when Pearlman went to introduce himself to the band prior to one of their shows. Long time friend of Mick, Robin 'Banks' Crocker thought that Pearlman was just some random idiot trying to blag his way into the dressing room and he punched the unsuspecting Pearlman in the face. This unfortunate misunderstanding was passed off graciously by Pearlman.

The recordings were then postponed after only a couple of days when Joe was diagnosed with hepatitis and spent most of February in hospital. The sessions were eventually restarted and the album was recorded in a lengthy process starting in May 1978 at Utopia and Basing Street Studios in London. The recording was interrupted by live dates and disputes with the record company, but overdubbing and mixing re-commenced at The Automatt in San Francisco in August and finally at The Record Plant in New York City the following month.

27

Once in the studio, Pearlman immediately recognised Topper as one of the best drummers he'd ever seen, but the ever self-deprecating Paul knew that he himself was struggling, only having played bass for around two years up to that point. Pearlman coaxed the best out of him and the resulting level of musicianship is certainly adequate and up to the task, but Paul was self-conscious under what he described as the 'nit-picking' process and didn't enjoy his part in recording the album. Some sources claim that Mick actually re-recorded some of the basslines himself once Paul had left the studio. Mick certainly played all of the guitar overdubs and was taking a keen interest in the production techniques and overall sound of the project.

Pearlman's appointment caused some sneering derision in the trendy UK music press as he had an FM radio-friendly production sound and was thus decreed too mainstream for a punk band. *Give 'em Enough Rope* is indeed a rock album with a nice fat guitar sound and was therefore ignored or trashed by many commentators. This parochial musical snobbery has resulted in this album being unfairly underrated. In a way, the album can be seen as taking the original guitar-oriented direction of punk rock to its logical conclusion. As articulated in several of the songs, the band are clearly struggling with their ever-increasing fame, being sucked into the 'Rock and Rollercoaster' and wondering if they really are the last men standing up for punk idealism. The Clash continue to sing about their own experiences on this record, but the subject matter also begins to widen and develop in new directions, including more weighty geo-political sentiment than the first LP.

The artwork was designed by Gene Greif, who based it on an old photograph called 'The end of the trail'. It has strong, flat colours – a theme continued in the clothes worn by the band and the backdrops to live shows at that time. The back of the record sleeve states 'All songs arranged and performed by The Clash'. This wasn't true because the piano in 'Julie's Been Working For The Drug Squad' and the saxophone in 'Drug-Stabbing Time' are clearly played by other musicians. The Clash appeared to be trying to cover their tracks by not properly crediting these contributions. Perhaps they were over-sensitive about the possibly negative reaction of the 'Punk Police' aka the music press back home. They need not have bothered because the UK music press slagged off the album anyway. The public didn't agree and the album reached #2 in the UK charts, and they were right – *Give 'em Enough Rope* is a great rock 'n' roll record.

Side One
'Safe European Home' (Strummer/Jones) Lead vocal – Joe
BANG – like a gunshot – and we're in. No fucking about. The reversed reverb on the snare hits like a bullet between the eyes and the band launch into 'Safe European Home'. 'Where d'ya go?' asks Mick as Joe describes going to Jamaica – a place '...where every white face is an invitation to robbery...' Feeling like a 'Martian arrival' from another planet the singer is trying to

score without getting killed in the process. Non-stop energy with a two-tone siren guitar wailing through the verses. As with most Clash recordings, Mick and Joe's guitars are panned to opposite speakers, but with 'Safe European Home' Mick's overdubs fatten it up to an audio onslaught of vitality and power. The wall-of-sound breaks down into a backbeat/reggae guitar in a rock arrangement as Strummer ad-libs to the climax while Jones goes through a list of adjectives to describe his safe European home. What an opener for the album – just fantastic.

'English Civil War' (Trad. Arr Strummer/Jones) Lead vocal – Joe
The Clash move into anti-militarist politics with 'English Civil War'. This was the second single released from *Give 'em Enough Rope* with a re-working of the traditional American Civil War song 'When Johnny Comes Marching Home'. The easily recognisable melody is augmented by the lyric which slightly wrong-foots the listener by referring to the 'Underground' (which is the name of the subterranean railway that serves London) in the second line. Strummer puts the jingoistic lyric of the original on its head when a mother sees her son's face 'beaten to bits' by 'clubs and fists'. The musical punctuation keeps the edge on the excellent tune so that Joe can emphasise his lyrics and say what he needs to say. 'English Civil War' is not about the 17th century conflict that led to regicide and a brief English Republic – but more an updating of a fine old folk tune into late 20th century England where the country was choosing between tolerance and racism. The Clash debuted 'English Civil War' at a Rock Against Racism [9] gig in London in 1978, so there's not much confusion about which side they were on. There's also not much doubt about The Clash's anti-violence stance as the song finishes by Joe spelling out the tragedy;

Get his coffin ready 'cos Johnny's coming home.

'Tommy Gun' (Strummer/Jones) Lead vocal – Joe
The first single from the *Give 'em Enough Rope* LP, 'Tommy Gun' is The Clash continuing with the anti-militarist theme. The title refers to the Thompson submachine gun which had been used earlier in the 20th century by gangsters and soldiers alike, and also a pun on the nickname 'Tommy' for a British soldier.
   Instantly recognisable, starting with Topper's machine-gun quickfire snare (he actually played this part in reverse and the tape was played backwards when the song was mixed, giving the drum the iconic 'sucking' sound) and going straight into thumping chords. The musical soundscape resembles a war zone, peppered with gunshots and explosions and features one of Mick's great punk 'two-note' Morse Code-style guitar solos. Even though it has no chorus, this was an obvious choice for a single, with the phrase 'Tommy gun' repeated before each new line – e.g. 'You ain't happy unless you got one'. (This was possibly an unconscious reference to Lennon's 'Happiness Is A Warm Gun').
   The 1970s was a time of terrorist bombing campaigns and military oppression around the globe, and Joe states his clear antipathy towards violence perpetrated by terrorists and despots alike.

We can watch you make it on the 9 o'clock news
Standing there in Palestine, lighting a fuse.

He had, however, flirted with terrorist chic himself by famously sporting a
'Red Brigade' T-Shirt on several live appearances, illustrating a willingness
to compromise a coherent philosophy for a façade of 'edgy' style. The song
suggests that terrorists are basically attention-seekers and not unlike Rock Stars
in this regard.

I'm cutting out your picture from page one
I'm gonna get a jacket just like yours – Give my full support to your cause.

Explosive guitars and feedback imitate the chaos of armed conflict as the rapid-
fire snare mutates into a military drum tattoo and Joe's desperate vocal takes
on the air of a lament on the associated waste of life.

'Julie's Been Working For The Drug Squad' (Strummer/Jones)
Lead vocal – Joe

After three in-your-face big fat rock songs, the album takes a surprising turn
with a rhythm and blues groove augmented with honky-tonk piano (originally
played by Al Fields but then overdubbed). This track is an early indication
that The Clash were beginning to (subconsciously or not) break out of the
straightjacket of orthodox punk. 'Julie' wouldn't be out of place on The
Clash's next genre-spanning LP – *London Calling*. An example of this comes
at the end of the chorus when Joe shouts 'Gumbo!' and Topper slips in a
New Orleans-style drum fill. Well-crafted and performed, the song is about
'Operation Julie' which was a UK anti-drugs operation that went on to bust a
large Welsh LSD factory in 1977. After a period of surveillance ('...someone's
looking down from that mountainside...') the authorities raided several sites
and discovered enough LSD to make literally 'millions' of acid tabs. 'There's
Lucy in the sky and all kinds of apple pie' sings Strummer, alluding to the
Beatles song. There's a lot of Strummer-esque humour on show as well, as he
sings to the university chemistry students involved;

You could have been a physicist but now your name is on the mailbag list.

The song is named 'Julie's In The Drug Squad' in some pressings.

'Last Gang In Town' (Strummer/Jones) Lead vocal – Joe
Just over two years into punk and the energy and anger was descending into
antagonistic infighting with various groups and sub-groups (referred to by their
tribal haircuts 'Crops'...'Spikes'...'Quiffs' etc.), kicking each other's heads in
on the streets of London –

And it's brawn against brain and knife against chain

But it's all young blood going down the drain.

The Clash were anti-violence and tried their best to stop it, with Joe trying to prise off the collective blinkers by name-checking punk, rockabilly, soul, ska, cajun and even zydeco as all being perfectly valid musical genres and having a place in 'the high-rise' inner-city.

There is an epic despairing sadness to this song and the punchy bass/kick syncopation invokes the atmosphere of late-night London streets brooding with hostility and malevolence. The recording was built around Paul's bass, lifted out of a great take. Joe's guitar is panned left, but it is Mick's guitar, playing the main riff on the opposite side that underpins the melody and drives the momentum.

The music press hated it, accusing The Clash of conceited arrogance by claiming to be 'the last gang in town'. Strummer would later categorically state that this is not how they saw themselves, but the idea resonated with their audience. The fact remains that The Clash were still spearheading whatever was left of punk rock and attempting to move it forward with some sort of coherent meaning. After another classic vocal ad-lib, the last word from the last gang is Joe expressing his frustration with the situation by cussing 'Bludclart!'

Side Two
'Guns On The Roof' (Strummer/Jones/Simonon/Headon) Lead vocal – Joe

Beginning with a guitar intro not dissimilar to 'Clash City Rockers', but even closer to 'I Can't Explain' by The Who, Side Two of *Give 'em Enough Rope* kicks off with Joe swearing a legal oath – referring to a recent incident where Paul and Topper were arrested for shooting racing pigeons from a London rooftop. The band mythologised the incident, trying to elevate it from idiotic criminality into some sort of clumsy anti-authoritarian statement, which had the effect of making The Clash look more like believers in their own hype than a band with something to say. It looked even more contrived and ridiculous when Paul and Topper had themselves filmed going in and out of the subsequent hearings at Clerkenwell Magistrates Court for the *Rude Boy* movie. Despite this, the song manages to transcend its moronic genesis to become a great opening track, consistent with the anti-militarist theme explored elsewhere on the album...

They torture all the women and children. Then they put the men to the gun
Because across the human frontier, freedom's always on the run.

The message is a clear condemnation of gun violence and legal dishonesty. Along with 'Safe European Home' and 'Tommy Gun', Joe's interest in geo-politics is continuing to come to the fore, illustrating his high level of education behind the everyman public persona. He burst a blood vessel while laying down a particularly passionate vocal take and can be heard saying '... blood in my mouth' as the guitar outro collapses into the next track.

'Drug-Stabbing Time' (Strummer/Jones) Lead vocal – Joe
Fast-paced and on the front foot from the off, this anti-intravenous drug song
starts with the mantra-like chorus about '…working on the Ford line / Paying
off the big fine' as a consequence. The song ends as Joe the narrator wakes
from his drug-induced stupor to see a set of shiny black shoes as he realises
that he's been caught in a police raid. With hindsight, it would seem that Joe
was writing about Topper's use of heroin (not common knowledge at the
time), which would eventually be instrumental in the band's demise. 'Nobody
wants a user / Nobody needs a loser'.

'Stay Free' (Strummer/Jones) Lead vocal – Mick
Mick Jones wrote this slightly wistful, nostalgic ode loosely around his adolescent
friendship with Robin 'Banks' Crocker ('We met when we were at school…') who
ended up in prison for a time. 'I did my very best to write / How was Butlins?
Were the screws too tight?' ('Butlins' being the name of a British holiday camp
and a 'Screw' is slang for a prison guard).

   Mick name-checks 'The Crown' (and Sceptre) public house in Streatham,
South London as the drinking establishment of choice. The lyric about
coming of age sees working-class friends start smoking, go dancing and
getting into fights, but also alludes to how Mick's love of music diverted him
from getting into deeper trouble. Backbeat rhythm guitar gives the song a
light feel throughout, up until the end, when after saying goodbye to his old
friend – 'Go easy, step lightly, stay free'. Mick's lead guitar drives the harder-
edged instrumental section to the finale and eventual fade out. The lyric is
not strictly autobiographical (e.g. Croker was incarcerated in Wormwood
Scrubs, not Brixton prison), but the general sweep and the ordinariness of
the experiences articulated tended to resonate with the audience, and this
song has remained a fan favourite.

'Cheapskates' (Strummer/Jones) Lead vocal – Joe
The music press were sharpening their knives for the backlash against The
Clash and the band could see it coming. Joe sees the hitherto sycophantic
media abandoning and distancing themselves from the punk movement 'Like
a load of rats from a sinking ship'. The band owed a lot of money to the record
company and lived modest lives, but they were getting slagged off in the media
because they had allegedly 'sold out' by signing to a major record label in the
first place. They must therefore (the logic goes) be wealthy hypocrites. The
opulence perceived and/or imagined by the hacks was not a reality, so Joe begs
to differ with their perspective, singing;

> Just because we're in the news you all think we're sinking rich
> And we've all got model girls shedding every stitch.

The minor key and occasionally dissonant lead guitar give the song a sense
of disquiet and unfinished business. 'Cheapskates' is yet another highly
underrated track from a great album.

'All The Young Punks (new boots and contracts)' (Strummer/Jones) Lead vocal – Joe

Every band has its creation myth. The main title for this one derives from 'All The Young Dudes' by Mick's favourite band – Mott The Hoople, while the sub-title is a reference to a concurrent record by Ian Dury & The Blockheads called *New Boots and Panties* (more about them later).

After Mick's vocal preamble, Joe describes his meeting with the 'passing yobbos' (Mick and Paul) that leads to the formation of The Clash. He also mentions the band's 'Manager' (Bernie Rhodes) with whom they were imminently to part company, and there is a dig at him and his mafia-like 'contract'. (A similar accusation was made by 2-Tone band The Specials when Rhodes went on to manage them. Their first single 'Gangsters' accuses him of overbearing coercion; 'Bernie Rhodes knows – don't argue!').

After a bit of self-promotion, the lyric becomes a plea for young people to live their lives now and not to get stuck in dead-end jobs.

You've got to drag yourself to work, drug yourself to sleep
You're dead from the neck up by the middle of the week.

Musically, the sense is one of tiredness and melancholy, a surprisingly downbeat song to end the album with – superficially similar to 'Garageland' but lacking the latter's sense of defiance. As the album fades, the message is to quit your dead-end job and to keep the faith as Joe goes in to one of his classic ad-libs, rhyming 'A half a pint of brown' with 'Camden Town' – excellent!

'Tommy Gun' (7" Single – 1978)

Personnel:
Joe Strummer: vocals, guitar
Mick Jones: vocals, guitar
Paul Simonon: bass
Topper Headon: drums
Gary Barnacle: saxophone
Steve Nieve: keyboards
Produced by Sandy Pearlman / The Clash
UK release date: 24 November 1978.
Highest chart position in the UK: 19
US release date: N/A

The sleeve to the single is a mock-up of an Arabic newspaper with illustrations of violence and oppression around the globe, but also includes an image of the embryonic peace movement in Northern Ireland – at that time championed by ordinary women.

A-side
'Tommy Gun' (Strummer/Jones) Lead vocal – Joe
Identical to album version (above)

B-side
'1-2 Crush On You' (Strummer/Jones) Lead vocal – Mick
By any standards this is a poor lightweight pop song, more reminiscent of fake 'New Wave' bandwagon jumpers like The Knack than a band as important as The Clash. It's also the first crap B-side which is a shame because all of their releases to date had been of a high standard. Mick had written it prior to forming The Clash and it is a good illustration of how the band may have sounded if Joe had never joined. It is nevertheless well performed (for what it is) with Mick on lead vocal. The Clash had recently parted company with their Manager, Bernie Rhodes and one narrative suggests that this track was released by the band to spite Bernie because he hated it so much. It was recorded in March 1978 at Marquee Studios in Soho, London.

'English Civil War' (7" Single – 1978)
Personnel:
Joe Strummer: vocals, guitar, piano
Mick Jones: vocals, guitar
Paul Simonon: bass
Topper Headon: drums
Produced by Sandy Pearlman / The Clash
UK release date: 23 February 1979.
Highest chart position in the UK: 25
US release date: N/A

The cover of the single was a still frame from the animated movie *Animal Farm* based on the book of the same title by George Orwell. This links in to the lyric

As we watched the speech of an animal scream
The new party army was marching right over our heads.

This illustrates the fact that, despite their tendency towards socialist ideas, The Clash had no more illusions about the political left than the fascists they opposed. The lyrics to 'English Civil War' were printed on the back cover of the record sleeve.

A-side
'English Civil War' (Strummer/Jones) Lead vocal – Joe
Identical to album version (above)

B-side
'Pressure Drop' (Hibbert) Lead vocal – Joe
The Clash cover a classic Trojan reggae song by Frederick 'Toots' Hibbert, of Toots & The Maytals, thereby tipping The Clash's collective hats to the influence Jamaican reggae had upon them (although this is a 'Ska/Rock' version). The original version of the song was in the soundtrack of the movie *The Harder They Come* which The Clash also reference in 'Safe European Home' and 'Guns of Brixton'. The Clash had first tried to record it at the same time as the 'Complete Control' single with Lee Perry in August 1977, but it didn't work out. This new version of 'Pressure Drop' was recorded in March 1978 at Marquee studios in the same session as 'The Prisoner', '1-2 Crush On You' and 'Time Is Tight'. It is the only one of the four that features Joe on lead vocal, possibly because he was still recovering from having been hospitalised with hepatitis the previous month.

'Cost Of Living EP' (7" EP – 1979)
Personnel:
Joe Strummer: vocals, guitar
Mick Jones: vocals, guitar, harmonica
Paul Simonon: bass, backing vocals
Topper Headon: drums
Dennis Ferranti: extra high vocal
Produced by Bill Price / The Clash
UK release date: 11 May 1979.
Highest chart position in the UK: 22
US release date: N/A

The *Cost Of Living EP* was mostly recorded at Wessex Studios in January 1979, although there are early versions of both 'Groovy Times' and 'Gates Of The West' dating back to the *Give 'em Enough Rope* sessions at Utopia and Basing Street the previous year. The band used studio time purchased and allocated for the *Rude Boy* overdubs to make some additional recordings. In contrast to the discomfort that Paul had experienced in the Sandy Pearlman recording sessions, and also in contrast to Joe's hitherto neo-Luddite attitude, Mick Jones had taken the opportunity to learn from the process of recording with Pearlman and had soaked up the technical details of audio recording and production techniques like a sponge. Bill Price recalled how with *The Cost Of Living EP* and the two subsequent albums, the band would often start with a live take and then, working from Topper's percussion up, the bass would be overdubbed to correct any errors and Joe would re-record the vocal. Sometimes this was because of technical issues, but often as not, it was because the final lyric was still emerging. When overdubbing vocals, Joe still wanted to play guitar simultaneously, even though the guitar might be unplugged. This gave a visceral quality to the impassioned delivery; however, it also posed some technical difficulty of 'separation'. (Joe later solved this conundrum by beating his chest when overdubbing vocals to bring the soul and spontaneity to the performance). Lastly, Mick would then take control of proceedings and (often in the absence of the rest of the band) he would overdub the harmonies and guitar parts to complete the recording. This method of working in the studio ran through the majority of Clash recordings from *The Cost Of Living EP* through to *Rat Patrol From Fort Bragg*.

Side One
'I Fought The Law' (Curtis) Lead vocal – Joe
This classic was originally written by Sonny Curtis of The Crickets but had been subsequently covered by several artists. In August 1978, Joe and Mick were putting down overdubs for *Give 'em Enough Rope* in San Francisco when this song performed by The Bobby Fuller Four came on the jukebox. The Clash began playing the song at concerts later that same year. They always had a discerning eye for songs to cover, but this one matched the band to perfection, and is now most widely known for The Clash's version which includes Topper's double triplet on the snare during the line 'Robbing people with a six-gun'.

Mick later recalled how at the time of recording, Wessex Studio did not have an 'echo chamber'. To achieve the right amount of reverb, microphones had been set up in the toilets and the flushing urinals can just be heard at the very end of the recording.

'Groovy Times' (Strummer/Jones) Lead vocal – Joe
In line with the housewife's consumer paradise lovingly parodied on the gatefold EP cover, this track is part satirical piss-take, part social comment: 'Groovy times have come to pass'. The terraces at English football stadiums had recently been 'fenced in' to prevent pitch invasions. (This disastrous error of judgement by the authorities ended tragically at the Hillsborough football stadium a decade later when 96 football fans were crushed to death against one such fence). The inside of the gatefold cover is a contemporary photograph of such a 'caging' of ordinary working people. The Clash drew a straight line between this phenomenon and the 'see-through shields' used by police to control rioting.

The arrangement has an airy Folk/Rock acoustic feel with Mick Jones playing harmonica which the sleeve credits to 'Bob Jones', This is Mick, humorously mocking his own effort as Dylan-esque. Meanwhile, the inside sleeve of the EP contains a spoof financial newspaper-style text containing song lyrics interspersed with nonsense Latin.

'The King of early evening ITV' is a reference to Bill Grundy who (in)famously hosted The Sex Pistols on his 6 o'clock show on Independent Television in 1976. Grundy started off by attempting to belittle the band and then clumsily made a pass at one of the female members of the entourage. What resulted is TV gold when guitarist Steve Jones called Grundy (amongst other things) a 'Dirty old man' and a 'Fucking rotter', having been goaded and encouraged by Grundy who had clearly made a serious misjudgement. The incident catapulted punk rock to the front pages of the tabloids and led to EMI dropping The Pistols with indecent haste. ITV dropped Grundy with similar expediency. Joe clearly found the incident comical and wove it into the fabric of this song, giving it a lighter feel than might have otherwise been the case.

Side Two
'Gates Of The West' (Strummer/Jones) Lead vocal – Mick

Mick had written a song called 'Ooh Baby Ooh' which appears on the Basing Street recordings for *Give 'em Enough Rope*. At some point, the song went through another incarnation under the title 'Rusted Chrome' and then finally emerged with a new lyric to become 'Gates of The West'. It was partly recorded in 1978 at The Record Plant in New York while the band were there mixing *Give 'em Enough Rope* (hence the lyric 'I made it all this way / From Camden Town Station to 44th & 8th') and then finished the following year at Wessex.

Jonesy sensed that The Clash were on the cusp of 'cracking' America – 'Not many make it this far' he sings in the second verse, describing the band's success as 'the perfect crime'. The Clash backlash was in full swing in the British music press who criticised the band for wanting to go to America after singing 'I'm so bored with the USA' on the first album. Mick was slightly mystified by this parochial negativity, saying 'I thought they'd be proud of us' (for having done so well). Along with 'Groovy Times', 'Gates of the West' illustrates a move away from the big fat guitar riff sound of *Give 'em Enough Rope* with more subtle arrangement and instrumentation. Both songs remained unreleased in America until they were issued on a 7" single that was given away free with the US version of *The Clash*.

'Capital Radio' (Strummer/Jones) Lead vocal – Joe

Also listed in some releases at 'Capital Radio Two' to distinguish it from the early version, this recording was made because the band discovered that the limited edition 'Capital Radio EP' from 1977 was changing hands for large sums of money as fans chased the few copies that were in circulation. This second recording doesn't have the raw off-the-wall feel of the first version, but this is more than compensated by the fact that Topper plays on this one and the musicianship is generally on a higher level. In line with the feel of 'Groovy Times', this version starts with a gentle acoustic guitar intro and then launches into a beefed-up version. There's also a (Topper-inspired) hilarious cod-disco outro that includes Joe ad-libbing 'Have you seen me dance? / I'm the one that I want!' – a reference to the song from the *Grease* movie soundtrack that was dominating the UK charts at the time. Most radio stations more or less ignored The Clash and didn't play their records on the air at all. This fact, combined with The Clash's refusal to make potentially lucrative appearances on TV shows like *Top of the Pops* or *The Old Grey Whistle Test* meant that The Clash were not a mainstream band. Joe later said that this permitted other bands to ride the post-punk 'new wave' and allowed The Jam to become the '...Suburban Sweethearts. Good luck to them – they worked very hard for it. But to hear The Clash you had to go somewhere a bit more dangerous and dirty – and I like that'.

'I Fought The Law (Reprise)' – aka 'The Cost Of Living Advert' (Curtis) Lead vocal – Joe

So with the sleeve of the EP looking like a box of soap powder, The Clash tacked an additional ditty onto the end of the original vinyl record. Joe puts on a fake West Indian accent and recites a mock advertisement for his product which is now available 'At your nearest Clash showroom'. This 'hidden' gem was added to the end of the 'Capital Radio' track but was not separately indexed or noted. Almost all re-releases under the title of 'Capital Radio Two' fail to include it, for example (and most inexplicably) this track was not included when the CD box set version of the 'complete' singles collection was released.

Sing Michael Sing

'London Calling' (Double LP – 1979)
Personnel:
Joe Strummer: vocals, rhythm guitar, piano
Mick Jones: vocals, guitars, bass, piano
Paul Simonon: vocals, bass
Topper Headon: drums, percussion
Mickey Gallagher: keyboards
The Irish Horns (John Earle, Ray Beavis, Dick Hanson): brass
Produced by Guy Stevens
UK release date: 14 December 1979.
Highest chart position in the UK: 9
US release date: 21 January 1980.
Highest chart position in the US: 27

The most widely recognised Clash LP with the iconic front cover, *London Calling* is what many believe to be The Clash's best album. Voted by *Rolling Stone* (magazine) as the 'Best Album of the 1980s', it was in fact released in the UK at the end of 1979.

The Clash had come back from the 'Pearl Harbour Tour' of the United States in February 1979, and after releasing *The Cost of Living EP* in May, they began rehearsing and writing *London Calling* up until August that same year. The band were hugely in debt to CBS and had now parted company with their manager (Bernie Rhodes – who had effectively frozen their income). After a few months, they asked 'Blackhill Management' to look after their business affairs and were assisted in this regard by their new 'fixer', Kosmo Vinyl. Homeless and broke, The Clash were looking for a new place to rehearse that was cheap and 'under the radar'. There was a sense of having their backs to the wall and that the band were writing for their musical lives.

They set up camp in fairly primitive surroundings at Vanilla Studio in Causton Street, Pimlico and began work. Not interested in going out to bars or nightclubs, the band just concentrated on writing and recording demos of the new songs throughout that summer. They played games of five-a-side football in between the music sessions and this appeared to have two benefits in particular. Firstly, it cemented their friendship – this was the period wherein they enjoyed each other's company the most. Topper would later describe this period as when the band were 'closest' as friends to each other – they played football as a team and took on anyone that was around. This was especially fun when representatives from the record company visited and consequently suffered a bit of over-enthusiastic tackling from the band. Secondly, the football sessions had the fortuitous effect that the band were nicely limbered up and ready to play music after a game. The resulting demos that the band had recorded themselves via a small mixer onto a TEAC recorder (a sort of primitive analogue 4-track tape recorder) were latterly known as *The Vanilla Tapes* and the legend goes that these demos were 'lost' by one of the crew, left on a train carriage somewhere on the London Underground [10].

Joe initially wanted to record the whole album by this 'punk' method, but reason prevailed and in August 1979 The Clash went into Wessex Recording Studios, Islington. They had asked Guy Stevens to produce the record which turned out to be an excellent choice. Stevens was more interested in expressing emotion through music rather than a technically perfect performance of the material, and his antics in the studio became the stuff of legend. He would smash chairs and jump up and down in the band's faces while they were still in the middle of a 'take', and he infamously emptied a bottle of red wine into a piano while Joe was still playing it. Paul loved the attitude and felt liberated by the experience. He had been working hard and his proficiency as a bass player had improved tremendously. It should be noted that working alongside Guy Stevens was Bill Price – a very competent engineer who understood and believed in The Clash, having worked with them on *The Cost Of Living EP* earlier that year. Price worked with Mick to effectively finish the production of *London Calling* once Stevens' energising input had shot its bolt. The recording of *London Calling* also gave a proper platform for Topper to move beyond straight forward 'rock' and to demonstrate his impressive percussive skills. He usually arrived for an hour's extra practice before the others.

Jones and Strummer were now writing and performing better than ever, but the key to the glory of *London Calling* was the opening up of the band's musical horizons. They had now been to the birthplace of rock and roll and were in the process of taking their music to the next level. Mickey Gallagher from Ian Dury & The Blockheads had just been on tour with The Clash, so he was invited to play keyboards for the recordings and stayed with the band for the subsequent '16 Tons' tour.

Having established their punk credentials in 1976 through the Stalinist/Maoist 'Year-Zero' philosophy of punk, The Clash broke out of the musical straitjacket and embraced wider horizons with *London Calling*. Despite the trashing of the old 'dinosaurs' of rock at the outset, the clues are there in The Clash's early work to indicate a deep rooted love of the work of their American and British predecessors. The ethos of punk now put forward by The Clash was that you should be able to play whatever kind of music you wanted to. So while most punk bands were busy 'painting themselves into a corner', The Clash were going where the music took them with nothing off-limits and the result was an album that exudes passion and joy but with that crucial cutting edge that is essential for a great rock and roll record. *London Calling* was also to be the last album that The Clash made having written most of the songs for the album prior to recording, although some tracks do not appear on *The Vanilla Tapes* which indicates that they were written during the recording process.

There were eighteen tracks recorded for the album – clearly too many for a single LP. The Clash had asked for the album to be released as a double LP, but wanted the price to be the same as a single LP. The record company refused. A compromise was agreed and CBS allowed *London Calling* to be released as a single LP with a free 12" single and conceded that this could retail at the same price as a single LP. Once the deal was agreed, The Clash went ahead and simply released it as a double LP for the price of a single LP. This gesture was greatly appreciated by Clash fans who reciprocated with loyalty towards a band that really did seem to care about them. With 18 tracks recorded, The Clash left Bill Price to mix the album and immediately took off for America to play some scheduled concerts.

The photographer Pennie Smith had been with The Clash for the tour of the USA that preceded the recording of *London Calling*. It was her photos of the band that graced the inside sleeve of the LP along with the lyrics. She published her photographs of the tour in her book *The Clash – Before and After*. It was Smith that took the photograph that became the front cover. She explained that at that particular gig at the Palladium in New York in September 1979, she was watching Paul all night as he appeared 'edgy' – dissatisfied with the lack of atmosphere at an all-seated venue where the 'bouncers' were preventing the audience from standing up and dancing. Clearly agitated, Paul began moving in the general direction of Smith who began backing away but kept shooting (hence the image being slightly out of focus). In a fit of rage, Paul smashed up his Fender Precision bass and the moment was captured by Smith to become one of the defining images of rock and roll. When the artist and graphic designer Ray Lowry designed the album cover, he deliberately mimicked the first rock and roll record – *Elvis Presley* by Elvis Presley. On this album cover, Elvis is seen in a black and white image, holding his guitar up. On *London Calling*, the same type face design is used, but this time with the guitar smashing down. Pennie Smith originally argued against the image being used, citing its technical imperfection, but Joe insisted. The photograph captures the raw emotion and energy of the moment, linking into the lyric in 'Revolution Rock' – 'Everybody smash up your seats and rock to this brand new beat...' In 2010 the Royal Mail issued a set of postage stamps with classic British album covers, and *London Calling* was one of those chosen, along with others including Bowie's *Ziggy Stardust* and *Let it Bleed* by The Rolling Stones.

In the 'Creditz' section of the LP inner sleeve artwork is a message to CBS crossing out 3 from 5. This refers to *London Calling* being the third release of the five album contract they thought they had signed (although the band found out later that they were in fact contracted for ten albums).

The openness of The Clash to influences outside of punk, the core values underpinning their philosophy, the increased standard of musicianship and the spontaneity of the performance culminated in a collection of great songs performed with exuberance and energy. The result was the incarnation of one of rock and roll's truly great records.

Side One
'London Calling' (Strummer/Jones) Lead vocal – Joe
As one of the best-known Clash songs from the best known Clash album, the opening title track pulls no punches. Instantly recognisable from the iconic thumping staccato Em /Fmaj9 opening chords penned by Mick, the sliding bass, followed by a machine-gun snare, we are straight into business with

'London calling to the far away towns...' – what a way to start an album. Joe adds a new twist to the internationally recognised BBC World Service preamble; 'This is London calling...'. This phrase was used by the BBC in the Second World War when transmitting to occupied Europe, to the empire and the world beyond. It conjures up the image of a beacon of free speech – a light in the darkness, broadcasting to the oppressed in all corners of the globe. Joe was no stranger to the BBC World Service, having been an avid radio listener in his early years. The Clash use this picture of a post-imperial capital reaching out '...to the far away towns / Now war is declared and battle come down'. Mick encouraged Joe to keep re-writing the lyrics to improve them, so several discarded verses exist in Joe's notebooks.

Into the chorus and the punctuated 4/4 rhythm moves into a syncopated backbeat as the lyrical tone shifts slightly to unfold into some sort of post-apocalyptic [11] transmission, bringing the recipients up to date. Climate disaster and impending famine are alluded to, alongside the singer's (post hepatitis) 'yellowy eyes' with Mick's 'backwards' guitar adding a sense of disorientation. 'A nuclear error' has just occurred (the Three Mile Island nuclear accident had happened in the USA previously that same year). It's a dissonant horror show wrapped up in a singalong tune to alert the hitherto sleeping populace to the new reality. The Clash don't have the answers

Now don't look to us – Phoney Beatlemania has bitten the dust

- they are in the shit just like everyone else and this is brought home with the catchy but fatalistic refrain

...but I have no fear – London is drowning and I live by the river.

We hear the collective pennies dropping as London fades away from us, broadcasting an SOS distress signal.

'Brand New Cadillac' (Taylor) Lead vocal – Joe
No sooner has the Morse code SOS from 'London Calling' faded and we are into a driving Rockabilly rhythm as The Clash put a new energetic twist on the Vince Taylor classic. Originally used as a band 'warm-up' and featuring a basic 12-bar blues structure in E minor, the song is a perfect marriage of punk rock simplicity to the American rock 'n' roll heritage that The Clash were now unashamedly plugging into (although Taylor was in fact British). The musical triumph of *London Calling* is rooted in the fact that The Clash are now no longer in the cultural straight-jacket of incestuous British punk rock, but have now embraced the trans-Atlantic cross-fertilisation that had served The Beatles and The Rolling Stones so well in the previous decade. The same band that brought us 'I'm So Bored With The USA' are now singing about a Cadillac – The Clash are evolving. They've taken off the musical shackles and are now unashamedly playing the music they want to play. This is still fundamentally rebel music, but now injected with a huge dose of joy, humour

and magnificent contradiction.

Topper was concerned that the take had speeded up and Paul apologised for making a mistake, but Guy Stevens loved it. His production alchemy has somehow captured the life-affirming energy of the band with an approach that tolerates and allows for minor mistakes and fluctuations in precision and tempo in the pursuit of a more worthy goal. Spontaneity, passion and energy are essential – technical 'perfection', less so. 'Cadillac' was captured in the first take. Only two tracks in and we know we're in for a new blend of the rock 'n' roll formula from a band at the top of their game.

'Jimmy Jazz' (Strummer/Jones) Lead vocal – Joe
Up until now, The Clash had (more or less) been a big fat guitar riff band with a bit of reggae thrown in for good measure but here is something different. Beginning with an 8-bar blues chord sequence over indistinct chatter augmented with whistling, 'Jimmy Jazz' gives us a change of tempo and an unexpected change of musical direction. The song is quite simple in construction, but the expert arrangement and performance keep us interested throughout. The lyric draws the audience in as we want to know what happens next in the narrative:

> Police walked in for Jimmy Jazz
> I said 'He ain't here but he sure went past'…

We are into a tale told by Joe as a slurring, semi-conscious witness answering to the authorities as the barroom piano tinkles away in the background.

Paul moves between punctuating to walking bass lines, and saxophone kicks in as the narrator exclaims: 'What a relief / I feel like a soldier – look like a thief!'

The Irish Horns make their first appearance on the record and as the soundscape gradually widens, Mick messes around with harmonics to add to the sense of disorientation as Joe switches between the English and American pronunciations of 'J-A-Zed-Zed-Zee-Zee-Zee'. Topper is right at home playing jazz from the light rhythms played on the rim, through complex cross beats and percussive variations on the kick drum and snare. He plays a 'straight 8' feel rather than the swing beat normally associated with the 8-bar blues format.

'Satta Massagana' is the title track of a reggae album by The Abyssinians released in 1976. The phrase itself means 'He gave praise'. In this instance, we give thanks for 'Jimmy Dread'. With understated brevity and a wry smile, Joe tells Jimmy 'I guarantee that it ain't your day – Chop! Chop!'

'Hateful' (Strummer/Jones) Lead vocal – Joe
The Clash had been with Bo Diddley on the 'Pearl Harbour' tour and were suitably impressed, so it was somewhat inevitable that they would incorporate one of his trademark shuffle rhythms into one of their songs sooner or later. After a great intro which includes Mick playing melodica over a dance-friendly groove, Joe starts to tell the tale with the opening line; 'Well…I've got a friend who's a man' The vocals move into the winning formula of Mick and Joe

counterpointing 'What man? – The man who keeps me from the lonely…'
At the end of the verses we hear a Strummer and Jones sing an increasingly
exasperated 'Oooow' before singing the chorus in unison;

> Anything I want / He gives it to me
> Anything I want / He gives it but not for free – it's hateful.

His 'friend' is, of course, his dealer and the singer charts his own gradual
decline as he loses his true friends to his own addiction. There is a pathetic
comedy to the tale as the narrator explains that '…it's paid for, and I'm so
grateful to be nowhere'. As the song builds, Topper's excellent percussion
is augmented with handclaps and at the climax, the subject spirals into the
repetition of 'Anything I want / Anything I want…' before the song suddenly
cuts off dead [12].

'Rudie Can't Fail' (Strummer/Jones) Lead vocal – Mick

Continuing with the Bo-Diddley-style rhythm but with looser syncopated
thumps interspersed with muted guitar strokes, Joe sets this one up after
encouraging Mick to sing 'On the route of the 19 bus…' (Joe took the number
19 bus from his girlfriend's home by the River Thames, past Pimlico and on to
Wessex Studio to record *London Calling*).

Thereafter, Mick takes centre stage with the Mick/Joe counterpointing vocal
exchanges reaching new levels of perfection as this next classic album track
gets going. A light-hearted finger-wagging lecture a la 'Message to you Rudy' is
given to our subject, who has been '…Feckless…Drinking brew for breakfast'.

'Rudie' was a character introduced by Joe during the vocal ad lib at the end
of 'Safe European Home' where according to that lyric, he had 'come from
Jamaica', and *Rude Boy* was also the name of the movie featuring The Clash
that had been shot around that time. ('Rudie Can't Fail' was the song that
played over the end credits).

'Rude Boys' or 'Rudies' were young men who were considered uncultured
outsiders, frequently associated with street-level criminality in 1960s Jamaica.
They were the subjects of comment by observers, alternating between
chastisement and sympathy. The Clash hooked on to the idea of the Jamaican
'Rude Boy' and his Anglo-Saxon equivalent in the British inner-cities.

The 'Rude Boy' subculture of sharp suits, thin ties and 'pork pie' hats was
adopted by the English-based Ska revival in 1979. This movement centred on
the '2-Tone' record label that featured homegrown bands including Madness,
The Selecter and The Specials (who had incidentally supported The Clash
on tour in 1978). The '2-Tone' label artwork was a design based around an
interplay of black and white imagery, indicating the racial and social mix
that was the basis of the movement. The musical cross-fertilisation between
The Specials and The Clash is particularly evident in 'Rudie Can't Fail' and
the sartorial influence became apparent as the Rude Boy style was partially
adopted into the 'look' of The Clash at the time.

'Rudie Can't Fail' features a Ska groove which verges on Rocksteady in terms of tempo, with a huge slice of Bo Diddley thrown in for good measure. It's a joyous and upbeat song and The Clash are clearly having a ball playing it. Their enthusiasm is infectious and the result is an outstanding performance of an excellent tune and a hugely uplifting end to the first side of *London Calling*.

Side Two
'Spanish Bombs' (Strummer/Jones) Lead vocal – Joe/Mick

Written in the studio and a jewel in the crown of *London Calling* – 'Spanish Bombs' is partly about the Basque terrorist group ETA, but is mainly about the Spanish Civil War (1936-1939) [13] and is an undoubted high point in the album. The melancholy lead guitar in the introduction paves the way for Joe and Mick to share the lead vocal in a somewhat sorrowful ode to Federico Lorca [14] and the doomed Republican cause. The Spanish Civil War drew idealistic volunteers from all over the world to join the 'International Brigades', set up to help defend the democratically elected socialist (Republican) government against Franco's anti-democratic fascist invasion.

> The hillsides ring with 'Free the people'
> Or can I hear the echoes from the days of '39?
> Trenches full of poets – The ragged army fixing bayonets to fight the other line.

Adolf Hitler assisted Franco, and the Luftwaffe's notorious bombing of the Spanish town of Guernica was immortalised in Picasso's painting of the same name.

Musically there is a gentle air of nostalgia and loss alongside the heartfelt lyric, because, although the song starts and ends with an A major chord, it consists mainly of minor chords throughout. The chorus, partly in Spanish, roughly translates as 'My love for you is finished / Oh my heart'. Mick was raised by his Jewish grandmother who was an infrequent attendee at Clash gigs. This song was her favourite – and who can argue with Mick's Gran? 'Spanish Bombs' is a lament for those who went before us and gave their lives to resist the fascist monster; 'My Senorita's rose was nipped in the bud'. The Clash pay tribute in the best way they can.

'The Right Profile' (Strummer/Jones) Lead vocal – Joe

Classic 'march' style and built around a relatively simple 8-bar structure alternating between the keys of E and B, the music for this track was jammed during *The Vanilla Tapes* sessions and recorded under the name 'Up-Toon'. On *London Calling* a lyric is added and a superb performance and arrangement transform this simple jam into a great song about a somewhat unexpected subject matter – the '50s film star Montgomery Clift. Clift appeared in several films (name-checked in the song), and was something of a rebel and a Hollywood heartthrob, but in 1956 he suffered a devastating car crash which caused slight long-term facial disfigurement, particularly on his left side (hence 'The Right Profile').

I see a car smashed at night / Cut the applause and dim the lights
Monty's face is broken on a wheel…

Clift remained dependent on prescribed sedative drugs and also self-medicated with alcohol for the remainder of his life. He became infamous for his erratic behaviour, and his health gradually deteriorated until his death in 1966.

The upbeat groove in the verses is lifted by the emphatic brass section while tension is added by a low, rumbling piano. An R&B saxophone solo sits over the instrumental verse invoking images of Hollywood glamour and positivity. While recording *London Calling*, Guy Stevens gave Joe a biographical book on Clift, giving rise to this lyric. Joe would later sing in 'Ramshackle Day Parade' 'All your life / Dreaming a dream / Somehow connected with the silver screen…' as the connection is made here between the dreams and aspirations of ordinary people and the resonances in the illusory fantasy world of stardom.

At the end of each verse is a two-bar percussive bridge by Topper that is different every time. Each verse brings us back to familiar territory in rhythmic terms, only to find ourselves tripping up again as the percussive bridges gradually seem to degenerate into more complex variations and triplets. This brilliantly illustrates Clift's gradual physical and mental deterioration. His descent into darkness is constantly juxtaposed with the light rhythms in the verses as Joe excitedly points out 'That's Montgomery Clift, honey!'

'Lost In The Supermarket' (Strummer/Jones) Lead vocal – Mick

On first listening, this sounds like a Mick Jones song all the way. He takes the lead vocal (which is usually a good clue) and the lyric appears autobiographical (like 'Stay Free'). This song is, however, a loving tribute to Mick written by Joe, who imagines Mick's childhood in South London. Mick would later disclose how when he was little, his parents fought much of the time and his Gran used to take him down into the basement to get away from it. They sat in this 'air-raid shelter' until the upstairs hostilities had subsided –

I heard the people who lived on the ceiling scream and fight most scarily
Hearing that noise was my first ever feeling. That's how it's been all around me.

The quick fix of materialism and the consumer's paradise (previously lampooned on *The Cost Of Living EP*) predictably transpire to be spiritually vacuous.

The song is notable in that it naturally sits alongside the typically English 'Kitchen sink' lyricists such as Ray Davies, Paul Weller, Alex Turner and Chris Difford;

I'm all tuned in – I see all the programmes
I save coupons from packets of tea.

Topper's use of the floor tom drum and subtle percussive skills continue to impress and there is a gentleness and a beautiful soft soul feel to the arrangement as a whole. Joe's tender backing vocals at the end possess a touching vulnerability as he empathises with the young Mr Jones.

'Clampdown' (Strummer/Jones) Lead vocal – Joe/Mick

'Clampdown' starts with feedback and an initial count in followed by a set of slightly confused and deliberately muddied sequences of descending notes, repeated over an ad lib vocal by Joe painting a picture of chaos and confusion – we realise there's a problem here. As the musical image before us comes into focus, the band ask 'What are we gonna do now?'

The drums keep the beat over a short pause with the question hanging in the air, and then Mick counts us in to a 4/4 old-school Clash foot-stomper. Topper adds urgency to proceedings as he leads the band, anticipating the first beat of the first syllable of the lines;

> Taking off his turban they said 'Is this man a Jew?'...
> They put up a poster saying 'We earn more than you'

What will *you* do if the fascists and racists start taking over? It's a question and a challenge to each individual to resist cowardly acquiescence to a racist regime where the collaborators will teach their 'twisted speech to the young believers'. It's a call to the idealism and confidence of youth to show courage and to take a stand the next time the neo-Nazis come calling 'Let fury have the hour / Anger can be power'. Mick takes over the lead vocal in the middle section, warning against the men that are 'old and cunning'. Topper simultaneously eases back and doubles up on the snare, the chords on the organ keep us in suspense and the guitar seems to be playing a Morse code distress signal like at the end of the album's opening track.

Then we're back in business, returning to the 'four to the floor' groove. Joe takes the lead vocal, warning against the appeal of the conservative older generation who '...grow up...calm down' and 'start wearing blue and brown' (fascist colours from the 1930s). It's a rallying cry to the young not to be taken in and become one of the de-humanised bullies kicking the shit out of those underneath them.

During the outro, Joe makes another reference to the accident at the nuclear power plant at Three Mile Island in Harrisburg, Pennsylvania, in 1979 [15].

'Guns Of Brixton' (Simonon) Lead vocal – Paul

Paul had been singing backing vocals but hadn't taken on a lead vocal until this point. He had this tune with its great bass line kicking around for a while and true to the alchemy of the rest of the LP, 'Guns of Brixton' came together in the Vanilla Sessions.

Overall, the guitars take a back seat while the accentuated bass and percussion come to the fore as do the dub-style sound effects (including a Jew's harp and the sound of ripping Velcro on the studio chairs). The street politics of the lyric refer to being arrested (a 'Black Mariah' was a police van used for transporting prisoners) and resisting arrest

When they kick at your front door / How you gonna come
With your hands on your head / Or on the trigger of your gun?

Paul references *The Harder They Come* – a Jamaican film starring Jimmy Cliff who wrote and performed the song of the same title. In the film, Cliff plays the main character 'Ivan' who meets his end in a shoot-out with police. What 'Guns Of Brixton' lacks lyrically it makes up for in the rootsy earthiness of the groove and Paul's half cockney/half Jamaican lilt vocal style. He was originally 'from' Brixton and attended Effra Road Primary School [16] and so he grew up around West Indian music and culture.

Unfamiliar with singing a lead vocal, Paul found it helpful during recording takes to direct his venom at an unfortunate record company representative who happened to be visiting the studio at the time. Joe played the bass when the song was performed live and Paul would play rhythm guitar and sing.

'Guns of Brixton' keys back into the street politics of the first album, but somehow updates them [17], dovetailing into the overall sound of *London Calling* and becoming an album high point and another fans' favourite, positioned as the last track on Side Two.

Side Three
'Wrong 'em Boyo' (Alphanso) Lead vocal – Joe
After an 8-bar blues introduction in C (and thereby leaning heavily on the 1967 version of the tune by The Rulers), The Clash make another foray into Ska, but this time by shifting into 12-bar blues structure with a key change thrown in for good measure. The folklore tale of the shooting of Billy (Lyons) by Stagger Lee in St. Louis, Missouri had been circulating in American music for most of the 20th century with various embellishments. The narrative usually involves the protagonists as small-time crooks in a gambling dispute that got out of hand.

A companion to 'Rudie can't fail', this arrangement features Mickey Gallagher and The Irish Horns centre stage, while Paul Simonon's walking bass and Topper's snappy percussion give the song its upbeat drive.

'Death Or Glory' (Strummer/Jones) Lead vocal – Joe
A stand out tune from *London Calling*, but tucked away on Side Three, 'Death Or Glory' is – in a sense – the sequel to the collective Clash mythology from 'Garageland' and on through *Give 'em Enough Rope* to here. The song title invokes martial connotations relating to stubborn bravery – The Clash frequently flirted with military themes. The tune starts with a reflective-sounding instrumental intro in which the bass plays a haunting melody before we launch into the big fat chords of a triumphant-sounding instrumental chorus, and then after a typical Mick Jones-style pause...

Now every cheap hood strikes a bargain with the world
And ends up making payments on a sofa or a girl...

The drums, bass and syncopated rhythm guitar underpin and accentuate the lyrics in the verses, with thumping chords punctuating the chorus. Life inevitably involves compromise, so how are The Clash to steer a path that remains true to the principles to which they aspire? They already know that

> …every gimmick-hungry yob digging gold from rock 'n' roll
> Grabs the mic to tell us he'll die before he's sold
> But I believe in this and it's been tested by research
> He who fucks nuns will later join the church.

It will be a long hard fight, but The Clash are still up for it. The usual state of affairs is that 'Death or glory becomes just another story', but The Clash are setting themselves up with the impossible task of reaching out to a wide audience without selling their collective souls to the Devil.

'…the beat of time' relentlessly counts down the hours from the cradle to the grave, at which point all are called to account and to answer for their actions. Critics had been writing The Clash off either as 'sell-outs', traitors or (worst of all) just plain irrelevant. They had no Manager, no money and a hostile media, but The Clash are right at home as outsiders. Before the song ends we revisit the introduction again, but this time Joe sings wearily over the bass melody 'We're gonna march a long way / We're gonna fight a long time' The rebel persona suits them just fine, and with 'Death Or Glory', The Clash vow to see this thing through.

'Koka Kola' (Strummer/Jones) Lead vocal – Joe
Closer to an 'old-fashioned' Clash song than the rest of the album, but demonstrating maturity and musical proficiency, 'Koka Kola' is a warning to the cocaine-fuelled hot-shots 'in the gleaming corridor of the 51st floor'. Coming from the same place as 'Hateful' here is another song about drug use, but this time it's directed not at the disenfranchised poor, but at the wired executives in the skyscrapers where 'the money can be made if you really want some more'. This time Joe has the avaricious rich in his sights. The lyric is not without its humanity, is never preachy and is peppered with humour. There is a knowing assessment of the dodgy goings-on in London, Berlin and New York by the money-making elite. The point being made is that the instant highs resulting from nihilist hedonism through illicit drug use by the rich and powerful is just as morally debilitating for them as it is for anyone else. The less fortunate are left pleading for the abuse of power to be tempered at least to some extent '"Treat me nice" says the party girl'. The high-stakes power games backfire on the players as the subject of the song ends up '…leaping from the window saying "Don't give me this!"' Topper's percussive beats seem to accelerate as the coked-up subjects alternate between an already fast pace and a manic quickening as the next 'hit' kicks in. The morally bankrupt and brain-dead executive is only kept going because 'Coke adds life where there isn't any'.

'The Card Cheat' (Strummer/Jones) Lead vocal – Mick

The big piano sound and opening percussive lick sound like they are straight out of the early 1960s as this fantastic album takes another twist with a Phil Spector-type 'Wall of Sound' production. In an interview, Mick told how he double-tracked the whole song by recording everything twice. He commences his dramatic and pathos-ridden vocal: 'There's a solitary man crying "Hold me"' and 'The Card Cheat' takes the listener on yet another musical journey with its change of direction and pace. The grandiose piano sound and the trumpet fanfare (played by Dick Hanson) give a sweeping, epic feel matching the gravitas of the subject matter.

A card game is taking place between the Gambler and Death personified. The scene is set up where the former is attempting to cheat Death by sleight-of-hand, but he misses the point – the grave is inescapable and a reckoning is about to take place. With a glance over the shoulder to the opening track ('Wrong 'em Boyo') our subject ends up being caught out and killed.

Ostensibly a Mick Jones song, Strummer's fingerprints are all over the subsequent lyric:

> From the 100 year war to the Crimea
> With a lance and a musket and a Roman spear

– (now there's a lyric you won't find anywhere but on a Clash record), as 'The Card Cheat' links personal integrity with mortality and each person's responsibility towards those left behind: 'Before you met your fate / Be sure you did not forsake your Lover'.

Not present on *The Vanilla Tapes* and so presumably written in the studio, 'The Card Cheat' neatly completes the batch of songs on Side Three that consider the consequences of avarice and dishonesty on the perpetrator.

Side Four

'Lover's Rock' (Strummer/Jones) Lead vocal – Joe/Mick

'Lover's' rock' is a genre of reggae music with romantic content – but 'Lover's Rock' by The Clash is clearly not reggae at all. They merely borrow the name for the title of this song which is loosely based on the book *The Tao of Love and Sex*. Joe recommended that this is a good book to read '…if you're a boy trying to be a man.' The Clash's relationship with femininity had remained pretty much unexplored up to this point in their canon of work. The image of four tough-guy musicians from the mean streets of London had played very well to the overwhelmingly male gallery, and whether they liked it or not, The Clash were now part of the music business which was and still is deeply misogynistic.

'You must treat your lover girl right' – so sing Joe and Mick in unison. It's a gently persuasive attempt to encourage young men to take off the cultural blinkers around sexual inequality in the bedroom as portrayed in the vast majority of Western cultural baggage. It's about getting away from '…that grubby feeling…' and experiencing deep and true sexual happiness as equals. It's about contraception. It's about restraint and respect; 'Whoops! There goes the strength that you need / To make real cool Lover's rock'.

This is a great song – it is never preachy, but gets the message across nevertheless. The band sits in an easy-on-the-ear groove and then seems to pause for thought before tripping forward over the descending bass line augmented by piano every time the song's title is repeated. This same piano adds immeasurably to the arrangement – sometimes lightly and subtly playing in the background, sometimes upfront with an almost Jerry Lee Lewis-style use of the upper keys, but always adding syncopation and fitting seamlessly into the soundscape.

Kirsty MacColl once gave a female perspective as she sang

The boots just go back on the socks that had stayed on
The next time they see you, they treat you like dirt…

With 'Lover's Rock' The Clash attempt to nudge their male audience to be a bit more thoughtful than that.

'A genuine lover takes off his clothes'… sings Joe …'Know what I mean?' Once the narrative is established, and we move into the third verse, Mick's use of harmonics on lead guitar expresses the exquisite ecstasy of sexual pleasure. Joe observes that it's 'Ridiculous innit?' and as the outro picks up and shuffles us on to the conclusion, there's even a vocalised version of a disco-style syndrum added in for good measure. Punctuated with Strummer-esque humour throughout, the last thing we hear is Joe calling out 'I'm so nervous!'

'Four Horsemen' (Strummer/Jones) Lead vocal – Joe
Despite Joe's ironic sense of humour, The Clash were rarely understated and here they are aligning themselves to none other than the Four Horsemen of the Apocalypse. Driving their 'Death or Glory' ethos forward, they recount how;

They were given the grapes that go ripe in the sun
To loosen the screws at the back of the tongue…
They were given all the foods of vanity and all the instant promises of immortality
But they bit the dust screaming 'Insanity!'…

This is the latest song in which The Clash continue to build and reinforce their own myth – a project that started on their first album. There's even a little puzzle in the middle when the listener can try to figure out who's who in the lines

One was over the edge, one was over the cliff
One was licking 'em dry with a bloody great spliff
When they picked up the hiker, he didn't want the lift…

'Not to be taken as Biographical' says Mick in the 'Armagideon Times' fanzine, but the middle section ends with the line 'Four horsemen and it's gonna be us!' so there's not much doubt about the four individuals to whom this particular alias applies.

51

This is, nevertheless, another great song from a great album. It gets its momentum from the double bass drum beat under the offbeat guitar strokes during the verses. There is more Jerry Lee Lewis-style piano as the band thump through the Mick Jones trademark stop/start arrangement. Topper drives the extended outro with his quickfire snare and the song seems to collapse, setting us up for the next track.

'I'm Not Down' (Strummer/Jones) Lead vocal – Mick

The Clash's determination to see this thing through is again articulated, this time from the pen of Mick who defiantly sings 'I've been beat up, I've been thrown out / But I'm not down'. A self-affirming anthem for the doggedly tenacious.

Light rhythm guitar sits under most of the song interspersed with a Kinks-influenced descending phrase, but the end of each line is punctuated by heavier chords to emphasise the point being made. Mick recounts the knocks he's taken to get this far and reiterates his determination to continue. It's his turn to tell us he's not going to give in.

> On my own I faced a gang of jeering in strange streets…
> I didn't run. I was not done.

Only three years have passed since Mick started The Clash with Paul, but almost eight sides of long-playing vinyl later and they are as defiant as ever. With 'Four Horsemen' and 'I'm Not Down' they continue to write, record and perform with passion and purpose. And they're not done with us yet…

'Revolution Rock' (Edwards/Ray) Lead vocal – Joe

Originally written and performed by Danny Ray, who had himself borrowed from 'Get up' by Jackie Edwards (hence the double credit) and then augmented with lyrics added by Joe, this is yet another high point of the album. The version of this song on *The Vanilla Tapes* is arguably the best of that collection.

Originally intended as the closing track, it encapsulates the feel of *London Calling* with a joyous clarion call to The Clash faithful to '…smash up your seats and rock to this brand new beat', linking in to the album front cover photo and bringing the album neatly to a close (or so it was thought at the time).

'Revolution Rock' radiates an infectious, uplifting positivity in no small way due to Joe's outstanding vocal performance. The lyrics are in the same vein of mild admonishment as 'Rudie Can't Fail' and 'Wrong 'em Boyo', but this time, Joe appeals directly to the small-time crooks and organised criminals to change their ways and to join in the fun.

> It's food for thought, Mobsters
> Young people shoot their days away – I've seen talent thrown away.

Joe sings to 'All you loan sharks' and then the song breaks down with just bass, keyboards and restrained percussion, drawing us in until Joe re-launches with

'The organ plays – and we're dancing to a brand new beat…'

The momentum of the dub-style arrangement is driven by the rhythm section as Mickey Gallagher expertly interweaves sustained and staccato organ chords while the guitar and the Irish Horns bounce from speaker to speaker. As the track closes Joe takes time to look in the mirror and laugh with a spoof advertisement for the band harking back to *The Cost of Living EP* as he promotes 'El Clash Combo…Weddings, parties, anything – and bongo-jams a speciality!'

'Train In Vain' (Strummer/Jones) Lead vocal – Mick

It takes up until the last track on the third album before The Clash deliver a straight-forward love song (one B-side notwithstanding). 'Train In Vain' shouldn't have even been on the album.

London Calling had been finished and after playing a few dates in the US, The Clash were back in London making some last-minute final adjustments to the mixes and also recording 'Armagideon Time' for the flipside of the single. They were packing up and were preparing to go back on tour when Kosmo Vinyl came up with a plan that The Clash would provide a song to be given away as a free 'Flexidisc' with the NME (New Musical Express) music paper. They didn't want to take anything from the new album, but they needed another song, so Mick went home and completed 'Train In Vain' overnight and brought it to the band in the studio the very next day. There wasn't enough time to teach Paul, so Mick played bass. It was pretty much recorded in one day, just before they set off on tour.

It later transpired that the deal with the NME fell through, and so it was decided that 'Train In Vain' should be simply added to the album. However, there was a problem in that the artwork for *London Calling* had by now already been completed. As a consequence, 'Train In Vain' appears unlisted – tacked on at the end of Side Four – and was not mentioned anywhere on the sleeve or the label. The only reference to it appeared on the inner disc run-out section which stated 'Track 5 is "Train In Vain"'. It was given this title on the spur of the moment to distinguish it from Ben E. King's classic 'Stand By Me'. Coming from the hand of Mick Jones, the song is a great and unexpected foray into soul/pop. Instantly likeable, with a catchy tune and great lyrics, starting with 'You say you stand by your man / Tell me something I don't understand…'

Mick had been through a tough period in his personal life. Apart from having no money, he had recently split up with his girlfriend and his home had been burgled and his music stolen.

Now I've got a job but it don't pay
I need new clothes, I need somewhere to stay
But without all of these things I can do
But without your love I won't make it through.

Mostly written and recorded over a 24-hour period, and consequently sounding fresh and unfettered, the serendipitous addition of the distinctive

'Train In Vain' on *London Calling* somehow lifts the album as a whole and its surprise inclusion as a closing track leaves the listener on an undoubted high.

'Train In Vain' was released as a single in the United States on 12 February 1980 where it became the band's first hit, reaching #23.

'London Calling / Armagideon Time' (7" Single – 1979)

Personnel:
Joe Strummer: vocals, guitar, piano
Mick Jones: vocals, guitars, sitar
Paul Simonon: bass
Topper Headon: drums, percussion
Mickey Gallagher: organ
Produced by Guy Stevens / The Clash
UK release date: 7 December 1979. Highest chart position in the UK: 11
US release date: N/A

A-side
'London Calling' (Strummer/Jones) Lead vocal – Joe
Identical to album version (above).
The artwork for both the 7" and 12" singles shows a pair of 1950s teenagers playing their favourite records by...wait for it...Elvis, The Beatles and The Rolling Stones (see '1977'). *Highway 61 Revisited* by Bob Dylan is also on display as are The Clash's first LP and *Never Mind The Bollocks* by The Sex Pistols.

The video for the song was filmed on Battersea pier by Don Letts. Due to unforeseen delays filming didn't commence until the sun had gone down and the weather had turned to rain, but as luck would have it – this simply added to the atmosphere and visual appeal of the final result.

AA-side
'Armagideon Time' (Williams/Mittoo) Lead vocal – Joe
The Clash had returned to London after playing some concerts in the United States and went back into Wessex to make some final adjustments to *London Calling* prior to its release. It was at this point that 'Train In Vain' and 'Armagideon Time' were recorded, the latter on 5 November – this (being 'Bonfire night') was the origin of the use of firework sounds that appear on the record. After the introduction featuring a preamble by Strummer, the song really kicks off with the thought-provoking lyric 'A lot of people won't get no supper tonight'.

'Armagideon Time' is a superb reggae cover version and was released as a Double A-Side on the 7" single. It had been played by The Clash on the preceding tour and became a regular feature in their live sets thereafter.

Just prior to recording, the band had been discussing with Kosmo Vinyl (from their management team) that the perfect record is under three minutes long. Strummer had instructed Vinyl to stop the band if they ran over this time. At 2.58 you can hear Vinyl interrupting the recording by saying 'All right, time's up, let's have you out of there' and Joe rebuking him with 'OK, OK – don't push us when we're hot!' as the band went on to continue the take to 3 minutes 48 seconds.

'Armagideon' is a Jamaican word equating to 'Armageddon' (as used by Bob Marley in the song 'One Love'). On 27 December 1979, The Clash supported Ian Dury & The Blockheads in one of a series of benefit gigs named *Concerts For The People Of Kampuchea* to raise money for the survivors of the Genocide in that country [18]. Their performance of 'Armagideon Time' was included in both the movie and the subsequent LP.

'London Calling' (12" EP 1979)
Personnel:
Joe Strummer: vocals, guitar, piano
Mick Jones: vocals, guitar, sitar, melodica
Paul Simonon: bass
Topper Headon: drums, percussion
Mickey Gallagher: organ
Produced by Guy Stevens / The Clash
UK release date: 7 December 1979
US release date: N/A

Side One
'London Calling' (Strummer/Jones) Lead vocal – Joe
Identical to album version (above)

'Armagideon Time' (Williams/Mittoo) Lead vocal – Joe
Identical to 7" single version (above)

Side Two
'Justice Tonight' / 'Kick It Over' (Williams/Mittoo) Lead vocal – Joe
The 7" version of the 'London Calling' single had 'Armagideon Time' on the flip-side. The 12" EP version had 'Armagideon Time' as the second track on Side One. 'Justice Tonight' running smoothly into 'Kick It Over' are on Side Two under the title 'Armagideon Time (Version)'. Both tracks are dub versions of 'Armagideon Time' with a louder bass and liberal use of reverb to give a more rootsy sound. This is The Clash's first serious excursion into dub reggae – and arguably their best. In 'Justice Tonight' Joe can be heard singing 'Use a calculator' – a theme returned to in 'One More Time' on *Sandinista!,* and 'Kick it Over' concludes beautifully with gentle offbeat piano. The 12" single sleeve credits are slightly different to those on the 7" insofar as they list Mick as having played melodica.

The original version of 'Justice Tonight / Kick It Over' from the 12" single is

8.51 in duration. On *Black Market Clash* it was edited down to 7.00 minutes. The original unedited version is available on *Super Black Market Clash* and the *Sound System* compilation.

'Bankrobber' (7" Single – 1980)
Personnel:
Joe Strummer: vocals, guitar
Mick Jones: vocals, guitar
Paul Simonon: vocals, bass
Topper Headon: drums
Mickey Gallagher: keyboards
Mikey Dread: vocals
Produced by Mikey Dread / The Clash
UK release date: 8 August 1980. Highest chart position in the UK: 12
US release date: N/A

A-side
'Bankrobber' (Strummer/Jones) Lead vocal – Joe
Mikey Dread was on the '16 Tons' tour with the band at their specific request, and in February 1980 whilst in Manchester (in the middle of the tour) they booked themselves into Pluto Studios and asked Mikey to produce this record. He got them to slow the tempo and along with Paul re-wrote the bassline. What resulted is a magnificent, lazy-paced reggae groove. Strummer is at the top of his game on lyrics and vocals while the band sit in the song like it's a hot summer afternoon. Joe's vocal delivery of the slightly doleful lyric is superb with his typical mix of melancholy and humour.

> My Daddy was a Bankrobber / But he never hurt nobody
> He just loved to live that way / And he loved to steal your money.

In the course of the '16 Tons' tour, The Clash had another madcap idea – a Clash Singles Bonanza. They decided to release a string of singles featuring new material at the rate of one a month. The first song selected for release was 'Bankrobber', however, CBS decreed that they would not release the song because it was 'not single material' and 'sounded like David Bowie played backwards'.

Both 'Bankrobber' and 'Rockers Galore' ended up on the B-side of 'Train In Vain' when it was released in The Netherlands in June 1980. CBS had egg on their collective faces when that single sold extensively in the UK as an import because British fans were desperate to get hold of the new songs. When CBS finally relented and released the single in the UK, it became The Clash's second-biggest hit to date.

A dub version called 'Robber Dub' was recorded for the 12" version of the single but due to the obstructive nonsense of CBS, remained unavailable until its inclusion on *Black Market Clash* the following year when it was partly spliced onto the end of 'Bankrobber'. The full version of 'Robber Dub' remained unreleased until its inclusion on *Super Black Market Clash* in 1993.

B-side
'Rockers Galore (UK Tour)' (Strummer/Jones/Campbell) Lead vocal – Mikey Dread

'This not black man's music – This reggae music!' Thus spake Mikey Dread when toasting with The Clash on the '16 tons' tour. Mikey was in the studio with the band while they were working on the Clash Singles Bonanza that morphed into *Sandinista!* 'Rockers Galore' is superficially a dub-style remix of 'Bankrobber', but this track has Mr Dread taking over the lead vocal completely. 'It no matter if you're slim and it no matter if you're fat'. Gently and with great humour throughout, Mikey points out that skin colour doesn't matter – a fact that we could still learn from in today's fragmented society with its ghettoised and divided culture. 'Whether reggae rocker or whether punky rocker…' music is for everyone. A great track, often overlooked and well worth seeking out.

Fucking Long, Innit!

Sandinista! *(Triple LP – 1980)*

Personnel;
Joe Strummer: vocals, guitar
Mick Jones: vocals, guitar
Paul Simonon: bass, vocals
Topper Headon: drums, percussion, vocals
Mickey Gallagher: keyboards
Tymon Dogg: violin, vocals
Norman Watt-Roy: bass
Mikey Dread: vocals
Other Guest Musicians: J. P. Nikolson, Ellen Foley, David Payne, Ray Gasconne,
Dave Yates, Den Hegarty, Gary Barnacle, Bill Barnacle, Jody Winscott, Ivan Julian,
Noel Bailey, Anthony Nelson Steelie, Lew Lewis, Gerald Baxter-Warman, Terry
McQuade, Rudolph Adolphus Jordan, Battersea, Luke, Ben and Maria Gallagher.
Produced by The Clash
Mixed by Bill Price and Mikey Dread
UK release date: 12 December 1980. Highest position in the UK chart: 19
US release date: 12 December 1980. Highest position in US chart; 24

Sandinista! is a masterpiece. A messy, sprawling, flawed masterpiece, but a
masterpiece nonetheless. To the newcomer, it may well appear unfathomable,
and this is where the format really matters. Remember that it was originally
released as six sides of vinyl with six songs on each side. 36 tracks – That's a
lot of music, so take it steady and listen to one 'side' at a time. If you listen to
it as individual songs, the rhythm of the music gets broken and fragmented.
If you listen to it as 2 CDs with 18 tracks at once, it makes no sense, so treat
yourself to a vinyl copy and get ready for a long but glorious ride. I promise
you it will be worth it. My main recommendation is that you listen to Sides
1-4 in any sequence you like – that really will be plenty to start you off. Leave
Sides 5 & 6 until you have been convinced by their predecessors. Some people
regard working their way through *Sandinista!* too much like hard work and
so they don't bother with it, but if the listener is prepared to settle in for the
long haul – either that or keep going back to it over a period of time, then the
rewards really are plentiful. There is so much music on this album and it is full
of little treasures that are easy to miss on the first few hearings. When people at
the time complained that *Sandinista!* was 'too long', Joe jokingly retorted 'It's
supposed to last you a year!' and Mick later said that he thought it would be a
good record for people on oil rigs or arctic stations.

To love *Sandinista!* is to love it, warts and all – and there are undoubtedly
some warts. Could it have made a better double-LP? – Probably, but that's
to somehow miss the point. Sides 1-4 are fantastic. Side Five has a few duff
tracks and side Six is more or less a dub of the whole album. But hold on –
just think how many bands have 'fillers' on single albums? One thing is for

58

certain – the buyer was not short-changed with this release — three albums for the price of one.

Recorded from February to September 1980 (between live shows) and at five different recording studios, The Clash and friends produced an album of astonishing diversity. If *London Calling* had widened the band's music to include Americana, *Sandinista!* blew any other musical blinkers away and nothing was off-limits. The album contains rock, rap, gospel, punk, jazz, reggae and so on. Mick was loving being in New York and was really into the emerging hip-hop scene there, soaking up the influences. Paul was away for the early part of the sessions, so Joe and Mick played bass on some of the original recordings and Paul did some overdubs when he hooked up with the band again later on in the year. The subject matter of Joe's lyrics are an astonishing mixture of street politics, social comment and world issues of the time – but again laced with a disarming sense of humour. Both his high standard of education and his global perspective (no doubt influenced by his father having served in the British Foreign Office) come to the fore. His interest in 'world music' was also becoming apparent – a rich seam he would mine again in future years with The Mescaleros.

After The Clash had finished the first leg of the '16 Tons' tour promoting *London Calling* they flew to Jamaica with Mikey Dread and started recording at 'Channel One' studio in Kingston. After only a short time they had a problem. Just prior to The Clash's arrival, The Rolling Stones had been in town and had been dishing out cash to keep the local gangsters sweet. The Clash went in after The Stones – totally oblivious, and were in the middle of recording when Mikey rushed in and told them that they had to leave immediately because there were some pissed off people on their way to slice them up for being 'disrespectful'. The band legged it out of town and Paul then flew to Vancouver for just over a month for his part in the previously arranged shooting of *The Fabulous Stains* movie project.

The rest of the band booked studio time at The Power Station in New York and started recording material straight away for the intended Clash Singles Bonanza (see below). In addition to 'Police On My Back', they recorded themselves messing about with other covers like 'Louie Louie'. Then they found out that Electric Lady Studios in New York was available, so they booked a three-week block straight away. They had almost no new original songs but started to feel their way with studio jams like 'Junkie Slip', (sharing bass duties between them) and in no time the mystical channel to the muse was wide open. With no manager to hassle them, they set up camp and immediately started pumping out track after track.

As with *London Calling*, the band worked hard in the studio, not going out and thereby avoiding distractions like nightclubs, but whereas that album had mostly been written prior to recording, *Sandinista!* was composed in the studio. Mickey Gallagher had been playing live with The Clash since *London Calling* and so he joined them in the recording studio and Norman Watt-Roy (also from Ian Dury & The Blockheads) was flown over from England to play bass, thereby adding his impressive skills to the blend. The stars were aligned and the music flowed out.

Joe installed some discipline in the process by building a 'Spliff Bunker' as far away from the mixing desk as he could. The bunker was constructed from flight cases with a slit-like a pill-box where the required headgear was an American war helmet. This meant that everyone could socialise and smoke in a designated area, come up with new ideas and keep the creative juices flowing whilst music was being properly recorded and mixed at a safe distance with some sort of sanity.

Other musicians were invited to get involved including Joe's friend from the '101'ers' days – Tymon Dogg, Ivan Julian and Mick's new girlfriend; Ellen Foley. Prior to *Sandinista!,* songwriting credits for original material were usually assigned to the authors, most commonly Strummer/Jones, mirroring the Lennon/McCartney-style arrangement of sharing the royalties between them even though some songs were essentially only written by one or the other. With *Sandinista!* however, things became a little more complicated. Topper was clearly contributing to the songs, and so the decision was made to credit all further original material to 'The Clash' on the record artwork[19]. This helped with band cohesion for The Clash, but also had the effect of sidestepping the responsibility of properly crediting other musicians that had clearly been involved in the production or composition of some of the material. The other contributors were either given 'Special thanks' and/or listed as 'Guest musicians'.

With Paul back on board, The Clash then played a series of gigs in Europe and The UK, after which they went into Wessex Studio in London to continue work on the album. Mick oversaw the project (assisted by Bill Price) as the band not only recorded new material but also continued to work on the large batch of songs that had already been recorded, most of which were at various stages of completion. Soon it became apparent that there were over 30 new songs available.

Earlier in the year, the original plan was to release the new material as 'The Clash Singles Bonanza' whereby the band would release a single a month over the course of a year, so that a new song would be released just as the previous one had peaked and was now going down the charts. Everything got held up when CBS initially refused to release 'Bankrobber' (they eventually relented and released it in the UK in August 1980), but then Mick taunted the record company by announcing that the new album would be a triple-LP retailing for the price of a single album. The band then realised that they didn't in fact have quite enough material for a triple album, so they decided to include tracks like 'Mensforth Hill' and the new version of 'Career Opportunities' as either 'fillers' or 'quirky/stupid tracks' depending on your perspective. Interestingly, they did not apply this lowering of standards to the B-sides of the singles released from *Sandinista!*

The Record Company were horrified at this proposal to release a triple-LP for the price of a single LP. As a consequence, the band had to forgo the royalties on the first 200,000 copies sold. Some record stores refused to stock it because it reduced their profit margins to what they considered to be an unacceptable level. *Sandinista!* was (at the time) a financial loss for The Clash, but a huge gesture of generosity towards fans. I don't know of any other band that has given so much music away for so little monetary return in the pre-digital era.

'The Armagideon Times #3' lyric sheet issued with the LP includes several very funny cartoons by the political cartoonist Steve Bell and the simple (and low-budget) album artwork includes a front cover photo by Pennie Smith taken near to Kings Cross Railway Station with Mick wearing a spliff-bunker type helmet. The colour scheme for the album artwork is an understated red, black and white [20].

The eclectic mixture of musical textures contained in this 36-track beast results in a collection of songs that the listener can return to again and again over the years and always find something new and interesting. *Sandinista!* will drag you out of your musical bunker and into the light.

Side One
'The Magnificent Seven' (Strummer/Jones/Headon) Lead vocal – Joe
The Clash had set up camp in Electric Lady Studios and had what Joe described as a 'scene' going on with fellow musicians popping in to add to the blend. There was a real sense of a collective endeavour and songs were pouring off the production line. They also happened to be in New York at the moment that Rap Music began to emerge as a distinct musical genre with the likes of Grandmaster Flash and The Sugarhill Gang. Mick, in particular, was soaking it all up like a sponge so when the *Sandinista!* sessions were underway, The Clash were keen to experiment. Mickey Gallagher and Norman Watt-Roy of The Blockheads were in the studio with Mick, Joe and Topper. Joe wanted to write a rap song, so Norman came up with the bassline. They recorded and looped the bass track and then Joe wrote the lyrics. Paul was in Canada, filming a movie at the beginning of the sessions, so it was Norman that played bass on this track. Rap produced a perfect platform for Joe to create this wonderfully

© Steve Bell

rambling lyric which starts with the daily grind and getting up for work in the morning

> Ring, Ring – It's 7am / Move yourself to go again
> Cold water in the face brings you back to this awful place…

- but then widens out to comment on the rat race in general

> Never mind that, it's time for the bus / We've got to work and you're one of us

- and consumerism in particular

> She's seen the ads, she thinks it's nice / You better work hard – I've seen the price….

'The Magnificent Seven' showcases Joe's irrepressible sense of humour wrapped up neatly in his rhythmic cadence 'Hong Kong dollar, Indian cents, English pounds and Eskimo pence'. Later, when asked what his favourite self-composed lyric was, Joe answered 'Vacuum cleaner sucks up budgie!' (which was taken from a tabloid newspaper headline), but the lyric also name-checks a shed-load of movers and shakers from the disgraced ex-President Nixon through Martin Luther King, Mahatma Gandhi and on to 'Plato the Greek and Rin-Tin-Tin'.

When played live, the chorus was a great chance for interaction between the band and the fans. As The Clash called 'You lot' bright lights would shine on the audience as we replied 'What?' It was another example of The Clash touching the hearts of fans in a way none of their peers could hope to. At well over five minutes in duration, this track was a long way from the two-minute punk thrashes on *The Clash*, prompting Joe to comment at the end 'Fucking long innit?'

'Hitsville UK' (Strummer/Jones) Lead vocal – Ellen Foley/Mick

'Hitsville' was the second single released from 'Sandinista!' and it sounds like no Clash record that predates it. If starting with a gospel-style organ into a punky bass line, then an almost nursery-rhyme sounding keyboard isn't enough to throw the listener, then the multi-tracked lead vocal by Ellen Foley singing in unison with Mick Jones is sure to do so. The lyric praises the DIY punk attitude managing to come to fruition through the development of the small independent record companies that gave rise to the 'Indie' genre. Several of these record labels are name-checked including 'Lightning…Small Wonder… Fast (Product)…Rough (Trade)' and 'Factory'. The Buzzcocks had started the ball rolling three years earlier with the *Spiral Scratch EP* which they recorded, manufactured and released without engaging with any established record labels. The lyrics of 'Hitsville' slam record company sleaze 'No slimy deals with smarmy eels' and describe the exploitative and parasitic nature of the industry as being filled with 'mutants, creeps and muscle-men'. The title is a play on the nickname 'Hitsville USA' used by Motown records.

Rock and Roll history is peppered with dubious moments wherein band members get their respective girlfriends in on the recording process, often with mixed results. In this instance, The Clash just about get away with it and the fact that Ellen Foley effectively takes the lead vocal and Norman Watt-Roy features on bass again provides another illustration of the sense of the 'musical collective' engendered during the recording of *Sandinista!* The sound of a female lead vocal was sure to wrong-foot many fans who initially struggled to comprehend the album, but despite the wide musical palette, the punk attitude underpins *Sandinista!* as illustrated in a lyric like 'A mike and boom in your living room' which harks straight back to 'Garageland' from the first LP. The Clash are having a musical party with *Sandinista!* and everybody is invited.

'Junco Partner' (Ellen) Lead vocal – Joe

'Junco Partner' was initially recorded at Channel One Studios in Kingston, Jamaica with Mikey Dread, and was incomplete when the band had to make a hasty exit from the local gangsters, so it was finished at Wessex Studio in London.

Starting with a stuttering introduction, the reggae groove is then set up by the rhythm section with offbeat piano holding the track together while just about everybody else goes off on a tangent. Joe's loose vocal style is complemented by Tymon Dogg's slightly out-of-tune violin, giving the whole track a folksy, ramshackle feel. The slightly dysfunctional spontaneity of the music expresses the state of welfare of the subject matter who is suffering from a sense of disorientated stupor as a result of years of illicit drug use 'He was wobbling all over the street'.

'Junco Partner' shows The Clash instinctively picking up an obscure song, making it their own and inserting it seamlessly into their repertoire. Joe had previously recorded a version of 'Junco Partner' with his band the 101'ers. On the *Sandinista!* recording he changed the lyric to include his girlfriend at the time, Gaby Salter

So I've got to pawn my ratchet and pistol
I'm gonna pawn my watch and chain
I would have pawned my sweet Gabriella
But the smart girl, she wouldn't sign her name.

On the 'Armagideon Times #3' lyric sheet it states that the writer was 'at present, unknown', but 'Junco Partner' was originally recorded as a rhythm and blues track in 1951 by James Waynes. Its authorship was then credited to Robert Ellen (possibly a pseudonym of Bob Shad), but probably derived from earlier material by various blues artists.

'Ivan Meets GI Joe' (Strummer/Jones/Headon) Lead vocal – Topper

This track was recorded at Wessex Studios in London. Topper wrote the music, played piano and was persuaded by Joe to sing the lead vocal, but this was under protest because Topper hated the sound of his own voice. Joe had

IVAN MEETS G.I.JOE

Left: 'Keys To Your Heart' was Joe Strummer's first record, made with pub rockers The 101'ers in April 1976.

Right: 'We went out and got our name in small print on the poster.'

The dawn of punk as The Clash support The Sex Pistols in Islington on 29 August 1976. *(Sony)*

Above: Joe at his sweaty, petulant best at the Elizabethan Ballroom in Manchester on 15 November 1977. Parts of the gig were filmed for the TV show *So It Goes.*

Left: 'Someone just asked me if the group would wear suits.'

The Clash's seminal first album (UK version) with cover design by Paul Simonon and Bernie Rhodes. The US version (released in 1979) omitted the tracks 'Deny', 'Cheat', 'Protex Blue' and '48 Hours', but replaced them with 'Complete Control', 'Clash City Rockers', 'Jail Guitar Doors', '(White Man) In Hammersmith Palais' and 'I Fought The Law'. *(Sony)*

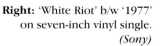

Right: 'White Riot' b/w '1977' on seven-inch vinyl single. *(Sony)*

Left: The *Capital Radio EP* on seven-inch vinyl, is now a rare collector's item – only 10,000 were produced. *(Sony)*

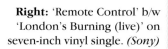

Right: 'Remote Control' b/w 'London's Burning (live)' on seven-inch vinyl single. *(Sony)*

Left: 'Complete Control' b/w 'City Of The Dead' on seven-inch vinyl single. A superb rock and roll record. *(Sony)*

Right: 'Clash City Rockers' b/w 'Jail Guitar Doors' on seven-inch vinyl single. *(Sony)*

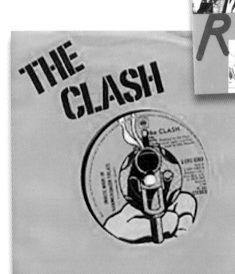

Left: '(White Man) In Hammersmith Palais' b/w 'The Prisoner' on seven-inch single. It was released in four different colour sleeves – blue, green, yellow and pink. *(Sony)*

Above: The poster advertising the all-night reggae showcase that Joe attended on 5 June 1977 and inspired him to write '(White Man) In Hammersmith Palais'. Shades of Lennon's Mr. Kite?

Left and below: 'Everybody's looking for the last gang in town'

Give 'em Enough Rope is The Clash's highly underrated second album. The cover predicts the rise of China as a military power. *(Sony)*

Below: 'White Riot' – The Clash play at a free concert for *Rock Against Racism* in Victoria Park, East London on 30 April 1978.

Right: 'Tommy Gun' b/w '1-2 Crush On You' on seven-inch vinyl single. *(Sony)*

Left: 'English Civil War' b/w 'Pressure Drop' on seven-inch vinyl single. The picture on the front sleeve is from *Animal Farm*. *(Sony)*

Right: 'The Cost Of Living EP'. It includes the rare track 'The Cost Of Living Advert'. *(Sony)*

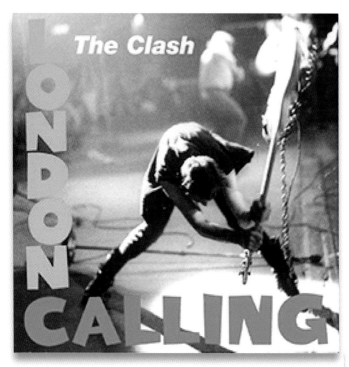

The Clash

LONDON CALLING

This page: 'London calling to the far away towns…'

The iconic cover for *London Calling* was designed by Ray Lowry who took the idea from Elvis Presley's first album.'Train In Vain' is not on the track listing. *(Sony)*

LONDON CALLING
The★Clash

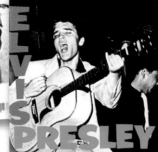

Right: 'London Calling' / 'Armagideon Time' – Double A-side seven-inch vinyl single. The twelve-inch EP has two dub versions of Armagideon Time, ('Justice Tonight' and 'Kick It Over') on side two. *(Sony)*

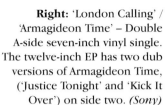

Left: 'Train In Vain' b/w 'Bankrobber' and 'Rockers Galore (UK Tour)' on seven-inch vinyl single. It was not officially released in the UK but sold extensively on import from The Netherlands as British fans tried to get hold of the new tracks on the B-side. *(Sony)*

Right: Mick sings 'Train In Vain' at The Lewisham Odeon on 18 February 1980. Mickey Gallagher can be seen playing keyboards in the background.

Left: 'Bankrobber' b/w 'Rockers Galore (UK Tour)' on vinyl seven-inch single. *(Sony)*

Right and below: 'The special mystery of music.'

The 36-track beast that is *Sandinista!* The accompanying lyric sheet 'The Armagideon Times no3' features hilarious cartoons by Steve Bell. *(Sony)*

Right: 'The Call Up' b/w 'Stop The World' on vinyl seven-inch single. This is the Clash at their most overtly political. The sleeve displayed the campaign addresses for 'Immobilise Against The Draft' in the USA and the 'Campaign for Nuclear Disarmament' in the UK. *(Sony)*

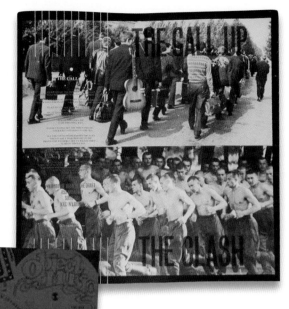

Left: 'Hitsville UK' b/w 'Radio One' on seven-inch vinyl single. 'Radio One' is credited to Mikey Dread. *(Sony)*

Right: 'The Magnificent Seven' b/w 'The Magnificent Dance' on seven-inch vinyl single. It was also released as a twelve-inch Single. *(Sony)*

BLACK MARKET CLASH

Left and below: *Black Market Clash,* a ten-inch mini-LP, USA only release. It was compiled to help US fans collect material that was unavailable there. It also included part of 'Robber Dub' and also 'Time Is Tight'. Both tracks were unavailable in the UK at that time. *(Sony)*

SIDE 1
1 **capital radio one** (2.09)
PRODUCED BY MICKEY FOOTE
2 **the prisoner** (3.00)
PRODUCED BY THE CLASH
3 **pressure drop** (3.25)
PRODUCED BY THE CLASH REMIX: BILL PRICE
4 **cheat** (3.06)
PRODUCED BY MICKEY FOOTE
5 **city of the dead** (2.27)
PRODUCED BY THE CLASH
6 **time is tight** (3.06)
PRODUCED BY THE CLASH REMIX: BILL PRICE
SIDE 2
1 **bankrobber/robber dub** (5.00)
PRODUCED BY MICKEY DREAD
2 **armagideon time** (3.00)
PRODUCED BY THE CLASH
3 **justice tonight/kick it over** (3.00)
PRODUCED BY THE CLASH & BILL PRICE

PHOTO: ROCCO REDONDO DESIGN: PAUL & JULEX

★THE CLASH★

The Magnificent Seven (5.40)
The Magnificent Dance (PREVIOUSLY UNRELEASED)
The Call Up
The Cool Out (PREVIOUSLY UNRELEASED)

Left: 'The Magnificent Seven' – twelve-inch vinyl E.P. It was not released in the UK. *(Sony)*

Right: 'Interrupting all programmes…'

'This Is Radio Clash' b/w 'Radio Clash' on seven-inch vinyl single. *(Sony)*

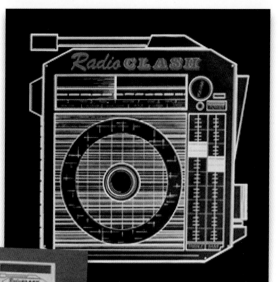

Left: '…resuming our transmission…'

'This Is Radio Clash' twelve-inch EP version. In addition to the tracks on the seven-inch single, the twelve-inch EP also included 'Outside Broadcast' and 'Radio 5'. *(Sony)*

Right: An example of a track listing from a bootleg copy of the 'lost' Clash album *Rat Patrol From Fort Bragg*. It was never officially released.

Left and below: 'The King told the Boogiemen, you have to let that raga drop.'

The Clash's last 'proper' album - *Combat Rock*. The cover photograph was taken by Pennie Smith who said that in the course of the photo shoot, she could see the band dissolving in front of her eyes. *(Sony)*

STEREO

1. Know Your Rights
2. Car Jamming
3. Should I Stay or Should I Go
4. Rock The Casbah
5. Red Angel Dragnet
6. Straight To Hell

1. Overpowered by Funk
2. Atom Tan
3. Sean Flynn
4. Ghetto Defendant
5. Inoculated City
6. Death Is A Star

THE CLASH
COMBAT ROCK

Right: 'Know Your Rights' b/w 'First Night Back In London' on seven-inch vinyl single. *(Sony)*

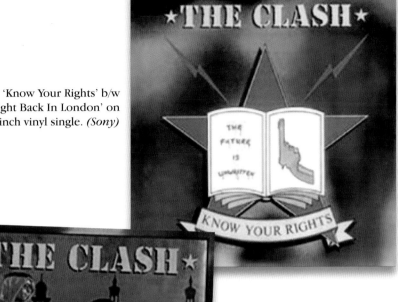

Left: 'Rock The Casbah' b/w 'Long Time Jerk' on seven-inch vinyl single. The twelve-inch version had 'Mustapha Dance' on the B-side. *(Sony)*

Right: 'Straight To Hell' / 'Should I Stay Or Should I Go' - double A-side seven-inch single. Although released as a double-A, radio stations concentrated on 'Should I Stay Or Should I Go.' The same two songs were also (pointlessly) released as a twelve-inch single. *(Sony)*

How to build your Clash collection

The best way to listen to The Clash is on vinyl, so the first five studio albums are highly recommended. If buying on CD, the most efficient way to get hold of most of The Clash's music is to buy the albums as a five-album box set, *The Singles* album and then *Super Black Market Clash*. The additional purchase of *Black Market Clash* involves some duplication but will add the essential 'Armagideon Time' and the original version of 'Capital Radio'. This very nearly covers all of the material they released while they were together. Do not buy *Cut The Crap*. *(Sony)*

Below: For completists, the CD format *Sound System* is well presented and more or less comprehensive, but pricey. It includes extras like outtakes and live versions, plus promo videos, early film footage, badges and lots of other goodies for the Clash fanatic. This is also the most comprehensive collection for downloading or streaming. *(Sony)*

written the words and it was Joe that added the sound of the games machines to the track after venturing out to the West End, ghetto blaster in hand to record the machines in an amusement arcade.

At the time of recording *Sandinista!* the 'Cold War' was in full swing and this song is a gallows-humour piss-take of the then current sabre-rattling / game of chicken between the USA and the USSR that threatened the whole world with annihilation. The insanity of the nuclear arms race based on the premise of mutually-assured destruction (which had the ironic abbreviation 'MAD') was simultaneously ridiculous and horrifying. Topper transcribes the posturing of the superpowers in an allegorical disco dance competition between Ivan and GI Joe.

The lyric name-checks the trendy clubs Studio 54 and Le Palace in New York and Paris respectively. This was one of Topper's first substantive contributions as composer with The Clash, and so it comes as no surprise that there is a dance feel to the track. When played live, Topper would take the lead vocal – the only time he was ever to do so with the band. With an eye to the future, the last verse declares 'The crowd are bored and off they go / Over the road to watch China blow'.

The theme was later taken on by the English band Frankie Goes to Hollywood with their classic dance record 'Two Tribes' in 1984.

'The Leader' (The Clash) Lead vocal – Joe

The lyric to 'The Leader' was inspired by the Denning Report on the risk to national security as a result of unwise sexual impropriety by a senior UK government minister known as 'The Profumo Affair' [21]. Illustrated in 'The Armagideon Times' by Steve Bell's hilarious anthropomorphic cartoon, the

© Steve Bell

lyric weaves a tale of the exposé in the media leading to a paranoid vendetta to shoot the messenger

> Have the boys found the leak yet?
> The molehill set the wheel in motion – His downfall picks up locomotion

Quickfire lyrics set to a rockabilly groove, 'The Leader' is a classic Clash track at under two minutes long but packing a disproportionately hard punch. The title is a pun on the leaders at the top of the political totem pole and the 'lead' story of a sleazy sex scandal so loved by the Sunday papers – 'The Minister knows his own affair'. The sexual peccadilloes of the elite ('...as he swings the whip from the Boer War') are nobody's business until they mutate into blackmail, corruption and the abuse of authority...

> The feeling of power and the thought of sex.

'Something About England' (Strummer/Jones) Lead vocal – Joe/Mick

Mick and Joe share the lead vocal by taking on the role of the two narrators of this sweeping account of England in the 20th Century. A play within a play, recorded at Wessex. The brass band (Bill Barnacle and Dave Yates) begins as Mick's narrator looks away from the detritus of a city centre at night and strikes up a conversation with an old man – an unwanted soul who has seen it all, but is now ignored by everyone around him. The old man, played by Joe explains that over his lifetime he has seen the rich shore up their own privileged positions whilst encouraging the poor to blame immigrants for this inequality.

Joe's character describes the Great War, the Depression, the Jarrow Crusade, and then the atomic age following swiftly after he returns home from fighting in the Second World War – 'all the photos in the wallets on the battlefield and now the terror of the scientific sun'. The post-war society 'fit for heroes' he was promised never quite crystallised and certainly never tackled the deep-rooted inequity of English society

> Through strikes and famine and war and peace, England never closed this gap.

The Music Hall piano tinkles away in the background while the troops sing 'It's a long way to Tipperary' and the ghosts of the two World Wars both bookend and haunt Joe's character. Mick's narrator concludes the vignette by returning home through the deserted streets to his bedsit with an unintelligible low cackle ringing in his ears. An extraordinary song, and an excellent ending to Side One.

Side Two
'Rebel Waltz' (Strummer/Simonon) Lead vocal – Joe

Side Two of *Sandinista!* starts in 3/4 time with a sleepy sounding guitar with heavy reverb. Light, ethereal piano comes in, followed by lazy sounding horns evoking a sense of otherworldliness. Joe wanted to experiment with a reggae bass in waltz time to illustrate the disoriented nature of his dream. Here is a wonderfully ambient introduction to Strummer telling us about his ghostly vision 'I slept as I dreamed of a time long ago / I saw an army of rebels dancing on air'. He sings a tribute to all of the fallen heroes, the idealists, the advocates of hopeless noble causes over the preceding centuries. Always one to stick up for the underdog, Joe sees the spirits of brave young rebels fighting out of principle to the bitter end

> A voice began to call / Stand until we fall / Stand until all the boys fall.

With echoes of 'Spanish Bombs', the singer knows 'the war could not be won' but is resigned to sacrifice his own life for a higher cause. In his final hour, he remembers his true love – 'In a glade through the trees I saw my only one'. The pitiless tragedy of the battlefield and the 'collateral' casualties of conflict are expressed poetically 'A cloud crossed the moon / A child cried for food'.

Incredibly sad and moving, but also somehow uplifting – sounding like nothing else in the world, 'Rebel Waltz' is a wonderful song that only *Sandinista!* could allow the space to breathe.

'Look Here' (Allison) Lead vocal – Mick
After a tongue in cheek a cappella introduction, Topper gets a chance to flex his jazz drumming muscles with this cover of a Mose Allison song from 1964. The bass playing sounds suspiciously like Norman Watt-Roy rather than Paul who was absent for a large portion of the *Sandinista!* sessions. Paul did overdub some bass parts at Wessex studios, but not unlike 'The Magnificent Seven', the performance on 'Look Here' has a distinct Watt-Roy feel to it. Mickey Gallagher is also busy cutting loose on piano, so the whole track is a joint Clash/Blockheads endeavour. Lew Lewis plays harmonica and there's also a marimba (probably played by Topper).

'The Crooked Beat' (Strummer/Simonon) Lead vocal – Paul

> Start the car, let's make a midnight run / Across the river to South London

So starts Paul's main writing contribution towards *Sandinista!* 'The Crooked Beat' is nicely tucked into the middle of Side Two. We have gone from a rebel's lament in 3/4 time, through a blast of fast-paced jazz and next on the list is dub reggae. *Sandinista!* can be difficult to keep up with, but this track sits perfectly into the running order of the album. 'The Crooked Beat' switches from 4/4 to 7/4 time and back again with the drums emphasising a different beat in each stanza, producing a meandering rhythmic feel. The bass line and stop/start percussion nevertheless set up an effective groove as Paul takes us back to 'the tower blocks' of his 'home town' of Brixton on the south side of the river, 'seeking out a rhythm that can take the tension on'. Although Mick and Paul ended up living in the Ladbroke Grove area of West London, they had both migrated there from South London (Topper was also originally from the South London borough of Bromley), so there's a wistful sense of homecoming and of wanting to get back to that music scene south of the river Thames.

> Take a piece of cloth, a coin for thirst for the sweat will start to run
> With a cymbal splash, a word of truth and a rocking bass and drum.

As with 'Guns of Brixton', Paul's monotone vocal style, somewhere between Cockney and West Indian does the trick of producing a street-level persona that draws us in with its authenticity. This track takes its time, but that is the point – it's a change of pace, a change of paradigm. What's more, about halfway through the track we are treated to our first dose of Mikey Dread. 'It's a bird? / It's a plane? / No! – It's a dub-wub styley…' and we glide smoothly into a dub version. The light guitars and sliding legato brass sounds are still present, but the cross-beats and rhythms are more to the fore – and that slightly crooked groove is driven on by the hypnotic bass line. But just as we are lured into relaxing back, Mikey surprises us again with a fantastic set up for a complete change of style and tempo as we move seamlessly into the next track…

'Somebody Got Murdered' (Strummer/Jones) Lead vocal – Mick

One of the more immediately accessible tracks on first hearing, Mick takes us from the opening sirens, via an arpeggio melody in an incremental build up into a straight forward 4/4 rocker. Whilst Joe was living near the World's End Estate in Chelsea, a parking attendant was stabbed for the sum of £5. Joe passed by the pool of blood on the ground and wrote this commentary on inner-city street violence where 'Somebody got murdered / Goodbye, for keeps, forever'. The song makes a sidewise comment on the strange combination of voyeurism and disinterest shown towards victims of serious crimes 'Somebody got murdered / His name cannot be found' while the media seek to titillate by concentrating on creating infamy for the perpetrators. It's a very human look at the distasteful rubber-necking that takes place in times of tragic news stories.

> As the daily crowd disperses no-one says that much
> Somebody got murdered and left me with a touch.

Whilst in New York, Joe had been approached by film orchestrator Jack Nitzsche who asked him to write a song to be used in his forthcoming movie project. Joe wrote the words, Mick wrote the music and the song was born, but Nitzsche never called back.

The dog barking on the track is Topper's dog, 'Battersea' (named after the stray dogs home in London). During the recording, Joe had to pretend to hit Topper in order to provoke Battersea into barking. The faithful hound's reward was to be credited as a 'guest musician'.

'One More Time' (Strummer/Jones) Lead vocal – Joe/Mikey Dread

Featuring Mikey Dread both at the controls and on vocal from the outset, 'One More Time' is an interesting take on a reggae rhythm with the piano and snare drum emphasising the offbeat and a 4/4 bass drum. It grooves along nicely with Joe singing about inner-city deprivation and violence but with an undercurrent of Strummer-esque humour, giving it a light touch feel.

> The old lady kicks karate for just a little walk down the street
> The little baby knows Kung Fu. He tries it on those he meets.

Mikey comes in again with his superb toasting vocal. Joe sticks to the subject matter with 'You don't need no silicone to calculate poverty' (harking back to an idea that first saw the light of day on 'Justice Tonight'). The lyric goes on 'Watch when Watts Town burns again' referring to civil unrest due to racial segregation in California in 1965 and then 'The bus goes to Montgomery', referring to the bus boycott in Alabama in 1955. Another highly underrated Clash song.

© Steve Bell

'One More Dub' (Strummer/Jones)

This is a dub version of 'One More Time' as would only be possible on a canvas as wide as *Sandinista!* 'One More Dub' sits neatly at the end of Side Two. Topper's drumming drives the momentum by initially emphasising every beat of the bar, then switching around between the third beat, and eventually onto the first beat and back again. Mikey's production involves intermittent heavy flange effect on the hi-hat and the use of heavy reverb provides a change in texture as the rhythm drives on. The second dub version outing of *Sandinista!* and a perfect end to the first LP.

Side Three
'Lightning Strikes (Not Once, But Twice)' (The Clash) Lead vocal – Joe

Twin track to 'The Magnificent Seven' and ode to New York City, 'Lightning Strikes' adds a funky twist to the rock/rap rhythm behind another set of Joe's quickfire lyrics, further showcasing his talent for verbal gymnastics. Written and recorded at Electric Lady during a thunderstorm, humour is never far away when 'Lightning Strikes in old New York' where 'The buildings touch Saint Peter's feet'.

Clearly enamoured by the Big Apple, Joe looks through a newcomer's eyes with awe-struck wonder and sees the wide spectrum of human existence from

Harlem slum to penthouse block / On every door I already knocked
There wasn't anybody that I didn't leave alone
Somebody lying under every stone

- and similar to Mick in 'Gates of The West' traces his own journey to 'Christopher Street' from

The Westway from Ladbroke Grove runs down to old Hounslow…
Just thought I'd mention the new extension
That runs down the 59th street intersection

A terrific vocal performance by Joe as the Clash/Blockhead axis comes up trumps again, driving the relentless momentum of the backing track. From the spoken-word radio 'phone-in' at the outset to the incessant snare strikes at the end, this is a burst of energy to kick off Side Three and another absolutely banging tune.

'Up In Heaven (Not only Here)' (Strummer/Jones) Lead vocal – Mick

After the initial transitional bridge that takes us from the A minor key of 'Lightning Strikes' through to A major, 'Up in Heaven' arrives to a more or less straight forward rock beat overlaid with a simple 5-note melody played on the lead guitar. This haunting phrase is used to introduce each verse but is beautifully absent half-way through each verse where the G-chord leaves us hanging in anticipation – the trademark of a Mick Jones composition.

'Up in Heaven' is a brilliant piece of observation and comment by Mick who wrote it about Wilmcote House – the high rise block where he lived for a while with his Gran at her flat on the 18th floor – one of 'The towers of London' common in the inner-city of the capital. After World War II there was an acute shortage of housing in London and the futuristic ideal of the tower block apartments was seen in the 1960s and early 1970s as the answer to rebuilding sufficient homes after Hitler's Blitz. The troops had come home to a new housing policy – 'reality estates that the heroes got'. After only a few years, the flaws in this strategy appeared as working class communities were broken up and fragmented in the de-humanising high-rise tower blocks.

The 'giant pipe organ' refers to the sound of the wind blowing in the Wilmcote House rubbish chute as the enforced social isolation leads to distrust of neighbours and strangers alike.

Fear is just another commodity here
They sell us peeping holes to peek when we hear
A bang on the door, resoundingly clear.

The final verse is a quotation from the Phil Ochs song 'United Fruit', pointing out that housing the working class by packing them into tower blocks has also happened elsewhere in other places and 'not only here'. The *'Alianza para el Progreso'* (Alliance for Progress) initiative by the USA in the 1960s involved financial assistance to Latin American countries in an attempt to resettle the poor as part of a well-meaning but ultimately doomed housing programme.

'Corner Soul' (Strummer/Jones) Lead vocal – Joe

Although the lyrics invoke Latin American imagery, 'Corner Soul' locates itself firmly in West London with the line 'They're searching every house on the Grove'. Ladbroke Grove appears several times in Clash music and iconography, but never with as much heartfelt passion as in 'Corner Soul'. On this occasion, the houses are being searched by the police – which is looking more and more like a precursor to an inevitably violent backlash. There are no fist-waving threats nor any call to arms here though – just a sad and sorrowful resignation that conflict is coming and that every individual has a decision to make.

Does it mean I should run with the dog pack?
Is that the way to be the one to survive?

In the verses, Topper's semi-military snare falls on the third beat while the bass drum plays four beats to the bar. In the chorus, the sound eases out of the reggae-based groove and opens out as Joe looks on and asks 'Is the music calling for a river of blood?' echoing the anti-immigrant 'Rivers of Blood' speech by right-wing British politician Enoch Powell some twelve years earlier. A beautifully melancholic piece with Ellen Foley's backing vocal blending in snugly to give the vocals the feel of sad lamentation.

'Let's Go Crazy' (Strummer/Jones) Lead vocal – Joe/Mick

Contrasting with and following on from the soul-searching in the previous track, 'Let's go Crazy' has a much more upbeat feel, but still the questions regarding participation in violent conflict are wrestled with. A fundamental pillar of the Clash's stated philosophy was that of antipathy towards violence, and so here the roots of the disturbances at the Notting Hill Carnival (as midwife to 'White Riot') are reconsidered. Beginning and ending with a recording of reggae musician Ansell Collins appealing for peace and unity at the Carnival, and set to a toe-tapping calypso beat, complete with steel drums ('Play on the pans'), the jovial atmosphere of a Carnival band is conjured up in a street party where 'Staring Dreads are jerking their locks'. There is a nice touch when, as the whistles blow, Mick delivers the line 'The lawful force are here – of course'. It's an audio pun because whistles were an old police method of alerting to danger, but whistles are also ubiquitous at the Notting Hill Carnival as a regular participatory addition to the soundscape.

'400 years of dread' refers to African slavery and helps to contextualise the parameters of inequality. This cultural baggage and institutional racism fuelled the mutual antipathy between police and black youth prevalent at the time which often manifested itself in street disturbances at the Carnival, particularly in the evenings. Clumsy police tactics when seeking to apprehend 'the sticks-man' (a petty criminal) frequently resulted in civil unrest, but this was just a catalyst. The damage had already been done in advance by the heavy-handed police tactics over the preceding year, so

The young men know when the sun has set / Darkness comes to settle the debt
Owed by a year of Sus and Suspect / Indiscriminate use of the power of arrest.

The 'Sus' laws were abolished in 1981 but up to and including the date of *Sandinista!* they effectively equated to stop, search and sometimes arrest with minimal evidence [22].

Despite the weighty societal issues examined in the lyrics, the overall feel of 'Let's go Crazy' is definitely celebratory. Mr Collins appears at the end of the piece with an appeal for calm and for peace, love and happiness as the steel band on the music float moves slowly away and into the distance.

'If Music Could Talk' (The Clash) Lead vocal – Joe
When The Clash recorded 'Bankrobber' in Manchester's Pluto Studios, they enlisted Jamaican toaster Mikey Dread as producer. 'If music could talk' was

© Steve Bell

born at that same session with a similar lazy reggae tempo. When they arrived at Electric Lady Studio, The Clash continued the project with Dread at the controls again. If it were necessary to reduce the essence of *Sandinista!* into one track it would be this one.

Joe's vocals are panned left and right as he ad-libs with a stoner's stream of consciousness touching on subjects as diverse as Errol Flynn, London Bridge, and the 'Special mystery of music'. The 'spliff-bunker' (where Joe skinned-up and wrote most of the album's lyrics) is also mentioned here.

'If Music Could Talk' is like a warm bath of music as Gary Barnacle's saxophone weaves in and out of focus. Simultaneously brilliant, beautiful and shambolic – easy on the ear, relaxing and rambling – a spliff-head's delight. The music reappears in a more dub style on Side Six in the guise of 'Living in Fame'.

'The Sound Of The Sinners' (Strummer/Jones/Headon) Lead vocal – Joe

Firing on all cylinders during the multi-genre *Sandinista!* sessions, Joe came up with the idea of recording a Gospel song. Featuring Tymon Dogg on harmonium and starting with the grandiose declaration over ringing chords 'As the floods of God wash away Sin City…', the song quickly picks up pace and enthusiasm with a 'Question and Answer' vocal with the 'congregation' repeating the counterpoint lyric 'Judgement day' to Joe's vocal ramblings of a spiritual pilgrim.

He clearly enjoyed playing metaphorical games with biblical themes (See 'Four Horsemen'). With 'The Sound of The Sinners' the drama is transposed to the 20th Century; 'I was looking for that great jazz note that destroyed the walls of Jericho', and Joe is also clearly having fun mixing up the themes of religion and drugs 'The message on the tablet was Valium'. He was to return to similar ideas years later with the Mescaleros (check out the excellent 'Get Down Moses').

It's unclear whether Joe is alluding to any personal epiphany or not, but he did once articulate the view that a spiritual solution is just as important as a social solution. From the deliciously venal, plummy voiceover by Tim Curry at the end it is clear that Joe is poking fun at established religious organisations, but with this track, he's also acknowledging the vein of Christian spirituality that runs through the early Blues music he loved so much. Either way, the playful humour shines through so that we don't get bogged down with negative scrutiny. The 'Sinners' are penitent and yet joyful and celebratory. 'After all this time to believe in Jesus / After all those drugs I thought I was him!' and finishing with the wonderfully caricatured ending of 'Lawd, Lawd, Lawd…'

Side Four
'Police On My Back' (Grant) Lead vocal – Mick

Side Four of *Sandinista!* kicks off with a stonking version of 'Police on my Back', written by Eddy Grant and originally released in 1967 by The Equals. From the opening two-tone siren guitar introduction, we are into a straight-forward rocker.

Recorded early on in the *Sandinista!* sessions at The Power Station, and one of the more immediately accessible songs on *Sandinista!*, 'Police On My Back' is the obvious single from the album, but true to the belligerent attitude of the band at the time it remained an album track only (although it was initially earmarked for the 'Singles Bonanza'). It was, however, released in the USA as the B-side to the less immediate 'Hitsville UK'.

Mick's great vocal combines with the thumping 4/4 rhythm to give a sense of urgency, while Joe harmonises during the verses. The standard backbeat keys into the natural cadence of the lyric in the chorus which simply and cleverly emphasises the offbeat. The lyric is subtly ambiguous regarding the guilt or otherwise of the singer. 'What have I done?' could be taken as a plea of innocence or just despairingly rhetorical.

Fitting so neatly into the semi-mythical Clash persona alongside 'I Fought The Law', 'Police on my Back' became another cover version that The Clash made their own. It was an immediate fan-favourite and was played at live shows right up until their demise and beyond (e.g. Joe Strummer and the Mescaleros' *Live at Acton Town Hall*).

'Midnight Log' (Strummer/Jones/Headon) Lead vocal – Joe
Another of Joe's quick-fire lyrics like 'The Leader', but this time put to a shuffle rhythm and focussing on individual morality ('Lines can and should be drawn') and white collar crime. Joe is cleverly pointing out the limits to what any system can do to bring the abuse of power to account

... Cooking up the books, a respected occupation
The anchor and foundation of a multi-corporation
... You won't believe me now but there's been some illumination
The wisest cops have realised they fucked the operation

Meanwhile...

To understand what's right and wrong the lawyers work in shifts

- so the singer tries to improve his understanding

I don't believe in books but I read them all the time
For ciphers to the riddle and a reason to the rhyme.

'Midnight Log' is a typical example of a superb lyric packed into a short song that is then tucked away on Side Four. Small treasures like this – understated and underrated - are undoubtedly what makes delving into *Sandinista!* such a rewarding exercise.

'The Equaliser' (Strummer/Jones) Lead vocal – Joe
Joe once described 'The Equaliser' as one of the main songs on *Sandinista!* A

dub reggae excursion, the bass and drums are the mainstay of the track with Tymon Dogg's violin contributing a certain sweetness to the brew. Guitar licks, syndrums and studio effects add to the mix and the music blends and works well. The song contains the most overtly 'Socialist' lyric by The Clash, arguing for collective action to bring about equality and wealth distribution 'Until half and half is equalised / Put down the tools'. As an audio piece, 'The Equaliser' fits perfectly into the collective thrust of the *Sandinista!* soundscape, but it doesn't really get going as an actual song. The repetitive nature of the melody works in the dub context up to a point, and the arrangement does assist in this respect, but the overall sense is one of unfocused ambience. The lyric is slightly clumsy in places and there's not quite enough of a song here, but a nice warm bath of music nonetheless.

'The Call Up' (Strummer/Jones/Headon) Lead vocal – Joe
'The Call Up' was the first single from *Sandinista!* and not like anything before or after. Starting with a warning alarm and a marching military count and then a gentle, steady groove as the simple melodic phrase is repeated over the semi-monotonous vocal line 'It's up to you not to hear the call up…' – an anti-conscription anthem. The guitars play variations on a simple D minor / C sequence that gives a sense of uneasiness and momentum throughout. Topper (who co-wrote it with Mick and Joe) plays xylophone and also drives the piece with percussion anchored into the integrated bassline, combining to unobtrusively underpin the steady thrust of the music. There is a sense of unsettled disquiet alongside the melancholy feel to the track to which Ivan Julian (of Richard Hell and the Voidoids) contributed on guitar.

The lyric goes on to condemn the historic sacrifice of youth 'All the young people down the ages / They gladly marched off to die…' for the greed of those in power 'Who knows the plans and why they were drawn up?' and on to point out that a potentially happy life with loved ones awaits those that can avoid the stupidity of war 'There is a rose that I want to live for / Although God knows I may not have met her'. The beauty of 'The Call Up' is in its steady, resolute message – not clumsy or aggressive, but soulful, articulate and tenacious.

'Washington Bullets' (Strummer/Jones) Lead vocal – Joe
The closest to a title track on *Sandinista!* and the most explicitly political song by a political band, 'Washington Bullets' sweeps seamlessly across a globe still in the grip of the Cold War. The song has a slightly repetitive melody in a relatively simple 8-bar structure, but it is beautifully arranged over Topper's marimba. Joe's highly articulate lyrics tackle international politics past and present, but the song actually starts with a reference to a street shooting in Kingston, Jamaica where some of *Sandinista!* was recorded (see 'Junco Partner'). The shooting of a fourteen year old youth by the '…killing clowns and blood money men' occurred just a few streets from where The Clash were recording. After focusing on this local tragedy Joe pulls the camera back to take in the bigger global picture – of superpowers fighting proxy wars around the world.

Strummer had been an admirer of Victor Jara, the Chilean folk singer who was mutilated, tortured and murdered by the US-backed Junta of General Pinochet after an anti-democratic coup that had resonances with the Spanish Civil War some 40 years earlier (see 'Spanish Bombs'). 'Washington Bullets' goes on through the failed CIA-backed invasion of Cuba in 1961 and on to the contemporary struggle of the Sandinista rebels in Nicaragua who – having ousted the hated fascist Somoza regime – embarked on hugely successful domestic programmes to improve health, literacy and welfare for the poor. The fascists retaliated with a terror campaign carried out by 'Contra' death-squads who were bankrolled by the USA (hence 'Washington Bullets'). At the time of recording in 1980, most ordinary people in the United States were uninformed and consequently unaware of their own government's role in this sordid affair.

When Joe spontaneously sang the single word lyric 'Sandinista' during the recording of 'Washington Bullets', Mick said straight after the take that this would be the title of the LP. In this way, the simple choice of a title for the album became a political act in itself – informing the public (particularly in the USA) about the atrocities that were being carried out in their name.

Joe doesn't let the left-wing off the hook as he lists depressingly similar conflicts around the world, including the Soviet invasion of Afghanistan

> If you can find an Afghan rebel that the Moscow bullets missed
> Ask him what he thinks of voting communist
> Ask the Dalai Lama in the hills of Tibet how many monks did the Chinese get?

Despite the weighty political subject matter, the song moves from an overtly melancholic start, through a quick history lesson and on to an absolutely joyous celebration of human endeavour in the face of hateful adversity. Joe even manages a sideways comic reference to *Fawlty Towers* (the iconic British sit-com) with a 'Que?' thrown in at the end to lighten the mood. 'Washington Bullets' is undoubtedly a high point of *Sandinista!* and is arguably The Clash's most underrated song on their most underrated album.

'Broadway' (Strummer/Jones/Simonon) Lead vocal – Joe

The Clash opened several live shows with this number, a trans-Atlantic companion to 'Something About England'. Ever so gently, 'Broadway' arrives and evokes a vision of a world-weary 'gentleman of the road' who engages in conversation. '"It ain't my fault it's six o'clock in the morning" / He said as he come out of the night'. Born poor, with a history of tough knocks '"I'm telling you this, mister – don't be put off by looks / I've been in the ring and I took those right hooks"'.

Typically for Joe, the song starts in a minor key while he sings the blues, but then moves to the related major in a stuttering, but gradual, upward trajectory (and juxtaposed to the social immobility hard-wired into the British class system as articulated in 'Something About England'). Consistent with the aspirational tales of the American dream, he imagines a future where he makes good and ends up '...driving one of those cars'. As the story progresses, the song gathers pace and our singer is now transformed in the emphatic crescendo of the finale as his irrepressible optimism sees him parading via a Strummer ad-lib 'Down the avenue... So fine... In style'.

(True to the particular atmosphere created by the *Sandinista!* mindset, the end of 'Broadway' then features a short recording of Mickey Gallagher's young daughter, Maria singing 'The Guns of Brixton' to a piano accompaniment. She sounds sweet enough – but the inclusion does detract from the ambience built up in the original outro of 'Broadway'. This is The Clash teasing the listener and deliberately undermining their own pomposity – Echoes of Lennon's cacophony at the end of 'A Day In The Life').

Side Five
'Lose This Skin' (Dogg) Lead vocal – Tymon Dogg
Written and sung by Joe's old friend Tymon Dogg, 'Lose This Skin' is not really a Clash song at all (Tymon released it as a solo 7" single in 1981), but was given a slot on the LP as a gesture of generosity in the *Sandinista!* collective endeavour. (Another view might be that it was included to fill the album with sufficient material for a triple-LP. Although the same could be said about the Mikey Dread crossover, the seam is somehow easier to see with this track).

The intro is set up by Tymon's violin playing sixteenths and then Topper brings in Norman Watt-Roy on bass and the groove is well and truly kicking. The shifting time signatures give the tune an unsettled feel, and sung by Tymon himself in own his distinctive way, the lyric is one of self-liberation. 'I've got to lose this skin I'm imprisoned in' – a sentiment very much shared by The Clash, although in this instance the wider lyric feels slightly exposed as it has to sit alongside Strummer's work. The biblical reference to 'The wife of Lot' is in the context of leaving somewhere and not being tempted to look back.

'Charlie Don't Surf' (Strummer/Jones) Lead vocal – Mick/Joe
After a slightly discordant piano sequence and helicopter blade sound effects, 'Charlie Don't Surf' eases in on a gently undulating bass riff reminiscent of rolling waves, before Topper cuts in to introduce staccato guitars in a superficially disarming pop song with a catchy chorus. This is The Clash sugar-coating the pill. Joe would say how humour and music could draw the listener in so that the serious point can be made. In this instance, the lyrical image painted is one of insular narrow-minded hostility towards people from other communities ('There's a one-way street in a one-horse town') and the fact that this mindset can lead to some very dark places.

Whilst in New York, The Clash began to rub shoulders with other artists, including those in the film industry. The connections with Hollywood's wilder contingent had been touched on in 'The Right Profile', but 1979 had seen the release of Francis Ford Coppola's epic movie *Apocalypse Now* with which The Clash were both fascinated and entranced. Based on Joseph Conrad's *Heart of Darkness*, the film is set in the Vietnam War and is a disturbing exploration of human morality in extreme circumstances. Themes addressed in *Apocalypse Now* were to reappear prominently throughout much of The Clash's work from hereon.

In a scene from the film which precedes a helicopter attack on a Viet Cong held village, the character Lieutenant Colonel William Kilgore played by Robert Duvall is arguing with a subordinate. In a somewhat surreal section of dialogue, Kilgore expresses his wish to see US soldiers surfing the waves whilst the battle is underway.

GI; 'I don't know Sir, it's err…'
Kilgore; 'What is it soldier?'
GI; 'Well, I mean it's pretty hairy in there isn't it? – It's Charlie's point'
Kilgore; 'CHARLIE DON'T SURF!'

('Charlie' was the nickname given to the Viet Cong by American soldiers).

'Charlie Don't Surf' is an exploration of the darker side of the human soul manifested in xenophobic attitudes towards other peoples and cultures from around the world. These same antipathetic attitudes anesthetise the public into complicity in the use of horrific and indiscriminate weapons such as napalm. This is expressed in the chilling lyric

Charlie don't surf and he'll never learn / Charlie don't surf so he's gotta burn.

It is also a warning against dismissing populist politicians in a sort of 'They laughed at Hitler too' sentiment. These people behave like idiots, so surely no one will take them seriously? But beware –

You can laugh and put 'em down / These one-way people gonna mow us down

'Charlie Don't Surf' is another terrific Clash track, tucked away in deepest, darkest *Sandinista!*

© Steve Bell

'Mensforth Hill' (Strummer/Jones)
By any standards this is a somewhat annoying filler. Critics of *Sandinista!*
can legitimately point to 'Mensforth Hill' as meaningless claptrap. Essentially
it consists of 'Something About England' played backwards with a few
embellishments – studio chit-chat, foreign language broadcasts, spoof police
radio traffic, sound effects and some vague notation. This isn't The Clash's
'Revolution #9' – it's a load of bollocks.

'Junkie Slip' (Strummer/Jones/Headon) Lead vocal – Joe
In interview, Joe said that some of the tracks on *Sandinista!* were being
written at the same time they were recorded. 'Junkie Slip' is definitely one of
these tracks. The band just started playing a monotone shuffling groove and
Joe ad-libbed an anti-drug lyric over the top. (Topper's heroin addiction was
worsening over this period). An unremarkable studio jam, this was one of the
first tracks recorded for the album.

'Kingston Advice' (Strummer/Jones) Lead vocal – Joe
The idea for 'Kingston Advice' dates back to the recording session started in
Channel One in Kingston, Jamaica along with the first takes of 'Junco Partner',
but it ends up sounding like one of the more directionless tracks on the
subsequent *Combat Rock*. The clumsy melody and a humourless, clunky lyric
are slightly improved by the song arrangement as the somewhat plodding track
progresses. 'Kingston Advice' sounds like a song that hasn't been properly
finished and is the last of a trilogy of tracks on Side Five that combine to make it
the weakest of all of the six sides of the original 3-LP vinyl format of *Sandinista!*

'The Street Parade' (Strummer/Jones)Lead vocal – Mick/Joe
The third of only four love songs by The Clash, and the only one of 36 tracks
on *Sandinista!*, 'The Street Parade' is a gentle Mick Jones tune with the
wonderfully appetising first lines 'I was waiting for your phone call / The
one that never come.' These lines are delivered with a touching vulnerable
melancholy over a quiet, steady background rhythm. The image is painted of
the unrequited love of a poor soul who sits in a quiet place while the carnival
continues in the near distance. After the understated percussion that underpins
the first verse, the rhythm section gradually lifts through a straight backbeat
with intermittent 4/4 bass to finally underpin the soundscape of steel drums
over a slightly cacophonous backdrop. We hear the music floats of the parade
pass by as our narrator becomes resigned to his romantic isolation and decides
to go outside to seek solace in anonymity 'I will…disappear and fade into the
street parade'.

Side Six
'Version City' (Strummer/Jones/Headon)Lead vocal – Joe
To get us ready for Side Six which features dub versions of other songs on
Sandinista! the announcer employs his 'received pronunciation' to introduce

'the old songs'. As he disappears, wistfully singing to himself the drums and harmonica fade in and we are into yet another underrated tune hiding in the grooves of *Sandinista!*

The laid-back rhythm and blues foundation supports a classic question and answer set up between the vocal and harmonica. Joe's slurring lazy legato adds to the amiable, easy-going Southern States feel of the music. The '…train from Version City' passes through the countryside interspersed with towns such as 'Gibson Town and Fenderville'. The singer assures us that the music of the Version train will take us out of The Blues and that 'She can pull you through to better days'. Another example of excellence on *Sandinista!*

© Steve Bell

'Living In Fame' (The Clash/Campbell) Lead vocal – Mikey Dread
Ever since touring with The Clash on the '16 Tons' tour, Mikey Dread (aka Michael Campbell) had been working closely with the band, including producing the 'Bankrobber' single. Although not as integral as Mickey

Gallagher, Mikey Dread was involved in producing and arranging *Sandinista!*, and with 'Rockers Galore' and 'Radio One' was not only credited with composition, but was also named as the sentient performer. The *Sandinista!* 'collective' spirit resulted in both 'Lose This Skin' and 'Living In Fame' being woven into the fabric of the album for Tymon Dogg and Mikey Dread respectively.

'Living In Fame' is a great dub version of the backing track of 'If Music Could Talk', featuring a warm bass under gentle percussion, and saxophone, guitars and keyboards liberally sprinkled with reverb. Easy on the ear and expertly arranged and performed by the ensemble with Mikey overseeing the chemistry, this is another hidden gem on *Sandinista!*

Mikey toasts over the top of the dub, name-checking punk bands like The Sex Pistols, the 'X-Generation' (Generation X) and The Nipple Erectors (latterly known as The Nips – Shane MacGowan's first band). Also name-checked are the new wave of 2-Tone bands including The Specials, The Selecter, The Bodysnatchers and Madness. Mickey Gallagher is specifically mentioned 'You've gone with the Blockhead' and Mr. Dread is as gracious as ever in his praise for his hosts and even gets a chance to have a bit of fun with metrification

Clash are ya ruler / Say a-Clash sound cooler / Say a-Clash sound sweeter…
Nowadays man measure a mile in a metre…Them, they measure gallon in a litre.

Joe tops it off with his backhanded complement at the end – 'Fucking Hell, Mikey!' before our spoof radio announcer closes the track, neatly bookending with the introduction to 'Version City'.

'Silicone On Sapphire' (Strummer/Jones) Lead vocal – Joe
This dub version of 'Washington Bullets' has Joe messing about with ad-lib vocals including random and nonsensical geek-speak panned left and right. The mix is a bit harsh on the ear and features otherworldly sci-fi sound effects that are intrusive to the overall sound. Nevertheless, the underlying music is great, and Joe's lyrics are again playful and a little bit silly as (for example) the voice in the right speaker says 'Go to RAM' and the left speaker replies 'Go yourself!' Paul once said that he didn't 'see the point of' tracks like 'Silicone On Sapphire', but it fits like a glove into the context of Side Six – mainly a dub of *Sandinista!*

'I am a Texas Instrument' is a pun on the name of the Dallas-based tech company of the same name and Joe Ely, a Texan co-conspirator who toured with The Clash earlier that year and was involved in the *Sandinista!* and *Combat Rock* sessions.

'Version Pardner' (Ellen) Lead vocal – Joe
It's 'Junco Partner's turn to have the dub treatment. The additional reverb accentuates the ramshackle feel of the original track with the bass cycle more prominent and even more hypnotic. It sounds like the boys were stoned when they put this dub version together – not always a bad thing, but there does

seem to be a lack of focus in terms of the arrangement. Having said that, this is a dub version of a fantastic song, well performed and well worth a listen.

'Career Opportunities' (Strummer/Jones) Lead vocal – Luke & Ben Gallagher

Joe said of *Sandinista!* that it contained some 'stupid' tracks and this one is a strong candidate. Sung by Mickey Gallagher's two boys (Luke and Ben) accompanied by their father on harpsichord-sounding keyboards, this is more or less just a simple but mildly pleasant karaoke re-arrangement of the song from the first album. Alongside 'Mensforth Hill', this is an obvious example of a 'filler' track to get over the triple-LP finish line.

Joe and Paul recalled having a conversation when The Clash first signed for CBS at the beginning of 1977 wherein they earnestly considered dropping 'Career Opportunities' from the set as they now had regular wages coming in. Fast forward three years and there is a sort of logic in the argument that the song had more relevance to schoolchildren than the band themselves. That said, the overriding sense is that we're now getting to the arse-end of *Sandinista!*

'Shepherds Delight' (The Clash)

'Shepherds Delight' is an instrumental based around an augmented dub from the same Pluto Studio recording session as 'Bankrobber'. The backing track is a strange amalgam of 'If Music Could Talk'/'Living In Fame' and the tune from 'Police & Thieves' with acoustic guitar to the fore playing licks as well as chords. Mikey Dread had bought some farm animal toys to play around with and they surface in this track. Another stoner's indulgence? Yes – probably. Another of Joe's 'stupid' tracks? Yes – certainly. Shepherd's Delight is a bit of a 'nothing' track and a strange inclusion on the album, given that the B-sides 'Stop The World', 'Radio One' and 'The Magnificent Dance' didn't make it onto the LP at all.

The track is basically over in two and a half minutes with another minute given over to studio chit-chat followed by a slightly incongruous explosion-ish (red sky at night...) sound effect with a long attenuated fade out – Possibly alluding to the launch of a nuclear missile. (Not quite 'A Day in the Life').

Sandinista! ends more with a whimper than a bang but despite itself remains a magnificent 'warts and all' flawed masterpiece.

'The Call Up' (7" Single – 1980)

Personnel:
Joe Strummer: vocals, guitar
Mick Jones: vocals, lead guitar
Paul Simonon: bass
Topper Headon: drums, xylophone
Ivan Julian: guitar
Produced by Bill Price / The Clash

UK release date: 21 November 1980.
Highest chart position in the UK: 40
US release date: N/A

A-side
'The Call Up' (Strummer/Jones/Headon)Lead vocal – Joe
(See album for full song review)
The Clash could have released 'Police on my Back' or 'Somebody Got Murdered' as 'safe' rock-format singles from *Sandinista!* and would probably have acquired more publicity and increased record sales, but the release of 'The Call Up' was both brilliant and brave. Here was proof that The Clash were relevant and that they still had something to say. (The sleeve reproduced the lyrics and also gave the address of the Anti-Draft Campaign in the United States). The video shows Topper dressed as an RAF pilot and Paul sporting military webbing. The look is still a mish-mash of styles reflecting the genre-defying album from which 'The Call Up' was taken. This is The Clash at their best.

B-side
'Stop The World' (The Clash) Lead vocal – Joe
B-side to 'The Call Up' and continuing with the anti-militaristic theme of the A-side, 'Stop The World' is one of the real hidden gems in The Clash's canon of work. It may be relatively unknown, but this track is well worth seeking out despite its slightly muddy production.

Joe was trying to work out 'Green Onions' by Booker T. and the MG's on the piano and while he was slowly shifting between F minor and Bb minor, Topper joined in on drums and the basic backing track was born. The simple two-chord structure is really just a vehicle for another of Joe's impressive sets of lyrics, and he is at the top of his game with this one – painting a picture of devastation in the aftermath of a nuclear explosion.

> The panorama of the city is wrong / In fact the city seems to be gone
> Burning rubber and smoke in my eyes
> There's a flat burning junk heap for twenty square miles…
> (while) Down in the bunkers in the crust of the earth
> Now crouch the wealthy and the noble of birth.

Written in the middle of the Cold War, the constant fear of worldwide nuclear annihilation was real. The more weapons in existence, the greater the likelihood of an exchange of atomic weapons initiated by mistake – human or otherwise

> There's some panel in a circuit board…
> Spotlit in a palace, shielded from dust
> Malfunction or not, the failsafe is the crux

and ending with the poetic images

The bank notes of Europe, the Emperors and Kings
Curl in the autumn as the burning of leaves
And I've cleaned my black guitar…

The sleeve of the 7" single included (along with the lyrics and the address of the Campaign for Nuclear Disarmament) a photograph titled 'The Dead Man's Shadow' showing a human shape outlined on some granite steps in Hiroshima where a human being was incinerated by the atomic bomb on 6 August 1945.

'Hitsville UK' (7" Single – 1981)
Personnel:
Joe Strummer: vocals, guitar
Mick Jones: vocals, guitar
Norman Watt-Roy: bass
Mickey Gallagher: keyboards
Paul Simonon: bass
Topper Headon: drums
Ellen Foley: vocals
Mikey Dread: vocals
Produced by: The Clash / Mikey Dread
UK release date: 16 January 1981.
Highest chart position in the UK: 56
US release date: 17 February 1981.
Highest position in US chart; 53 [23]

A-side
'Hitsville UK' (Strummer/Jones)
Identical to album version (above).

B-side
'Radio One' (Campbell) Lead vocal – Mikey Dread
In this made-to-measure B-side of 'Hitsville', Mikey Dread toasts over a dub reggae backing track that slowly and steadily draws the listener in to sit back and enjoy the ride. In the guise of a radio presenter reading the news, Mr Dread articulates his approval for the new independent record label movement. He admonishes the narrow-minded and blinkered approach of the powers that be for 'Finding a million faults of new products on new labels / Stopping a million sales by their fairy tales and fables'. He points out that 'The jury is in fury against Rockers on their turntables' and how in doing so they make 'I-man bawl'.

With a weatherman's hat on, he predicts 'Scattered showers of African smoke all over the studio'. The track is peppered with humour and you can almost hear Mikey's smile when as a result of 'herb smoking…The studio is cloudy, cloudy' just before he impersonates a stoned-out Strummer.

As with 'Rockers Galore (UK Tour)' Mikey extends the hand of friendship to all as music unites people in peace and love 'All over the nation / We deal with communication'. He announces that this is 'Dread at the Controls' (this was the name of his radio programmes in Jamaica and was also the artist's name for 'Rockers Galore' as displayed on the label of the 7" single on the B-side of 'Bankrobber').

'The Magnificent Seven' (12" EP – 1981) (Europe/US Only)
Personnel:
Joe Strummer: vocals, guitar
Mick Jones: vocals, guitar
Julian Ivan: guitar
Norman Watt-Roy: bass
Mickey Gallagher: keyboards
Paul Simonon: bass
Topper Headon: drums, xylophone
Produced by: The Clash
UK release date: N/A
US release date: 27 March 1981.

Side One
'The Magnificent Seven' (Strummer/Jones/Headon) Lead vocal – Joe
A remixed and brutally shortened radio edit of the album track.

'The Magnificent Dance' (Strummer/Jones/Headon) Lead vocal – Joe
A mostly instrumental 'dance' version of 'The Magnificent Seven', re-mixed by 'Pepe Unidos' (Strummer, Simonon and Rhodes). When released in the US, it received significant airplay in New York.

Side Two
'The Call Up' (Strummer/Jones/Headon) Lead vocal – Joe
Edited (shortened) version.

'The Cool Out' (Strummer/Jones/Headon)
An excellent instrumental version of 'The Call Up' remixed at Wessex by 'Pepe Unidos'. It has a clearer sounding production than its parent track and was unavailable in the UK until its inclusion on *Super Black Market Clash*.

'The Magnificent Seven' (7" Single – 1981)
Personnel:
Joe Strummer: vocals, guitar
Mick Jones: vocals, guitar
Norman Watt-Roy: bass
Mickey Gallagher: keyboards

Topper Headon: drums
Produced by: The Clash
UK release date: 10 April 1981.
Highest chart position in the UK: 34
US release date: N/A

A-side
'The Magnificent Seven' (Strummer/Jones/Headon) Lead vocal – Joe
Brutally edited and shortened from the album version.

B-side
'The Magnificent Dance' (Strummer/Jones/Headon)
An almost completely instrumental version of 'The Magnificent Seven', but at only 3.35 in length it is much shorter than the 12" version.

'The Magnificent Seven' (12" Single – 1981)
Personnel:
Joe Strummer: vocals, guitar
Mick Jones: backing vocals, guitar
Norman Watt-Roy: bass
Mickey Gallagher: keyboards
Topper Headon: drums
Produced by: The Clash
UK release date: 24 April 1981.
US release date: N/A

A-Side
'The Magnificent Seven' (Strummer/Jones/Headon) Lead vocal – Joe
A slightly remixed version taken from the album version but with around one minute cut from the end. A sheet of stickers was included with the release.

B-Side
'The Magnificent Dance' (Strummer/Jones/Headon)
A slightly extended instrumental version of 'The Magnificent Seven' re-mixed by 'Pepe Unidos' (Strummer, Simonon and Rhodes). Identical to the version released in the USA a month earlier.

'This Is Radio Clash' (7" Single – 1981)
Personnel:
Joe Strummer: vocals, guitar
Mick Jones – vocals, guitar
Paul Simonon – bass

Topper Headon – drums
Gary Barnacle – saxophone
Produced by The Clash
UK release date: 20 November 1981.
Highest chart position in the UK: 47
US release date: N/A

Sandinista! had received a good reception in the USA but the UK music press
slated it and were generally hostile towards The Clash. Around February 1981
Joe insisted that Bernie Rhodes be reinstated as band manager and Blackhill
Management were brutally dropped. Rhodes inherited a band that were
financially in a mess, but on a clear upwards trajectory, particularly in the USA.

Rhodes suggested the concept of 'Radio Clash' to the band. The basic idea
follows on from songs like 'Washington Bullets' whereby The Clash saw
part of their role as disseminators of important information not considered
newsworthy by mainstream media. Mick and Joe picked up the idea and ran
with it and the subsequent single was started in Marcus Music Studios in
London in April 1981, but not finished until November that year in Electric
Lady, New York (where Mick worked on the 12" mixes too).

A-side
'This Is Radio Clash' (The Clash) Lead vocal – Joe
The New York funk/rap scene had previously recycled the bass line from
'Rapper's Delight' by The Sugarhill Gang (which was itself derived from 'Good
Times' by Chic – also the origin of 'Another One Bites The Dust' by Queen).
The same glorious riff was unashamedly recycled once more to form the basic
groove for 'This Is Radio Clash'. Full of energy and a thousand miles away from
a two-minute punk thrash, it is the sound of The Clash enamoured by and
revelling in American music and culture. The reference to 'refusing all third
lights' relates to an old superstition from the First World War of never lighting
three cigarettes from one match.

'This Is Radio Clash' is a slightly crass and unsubtle trumpeting of the
Clash 'brand'. Although head and shoulders above its contemporaries, the
lyric lacks the humour of Strummer's usual work – the Hammer Horror intro
notwithstanding.

The video for the song was compiled from footage shot at Bond's in New
York by Don Letts for the aborted film *The Clash On Broadway* (see below).

B-side
'Radio Clash' (The Clash) Lead vocal – Joe
A rerun of the A-side 'This Is Radio Clash' with different words and a slightly
different mix, 'Radio Clash' has more humour and substance in the lyrics than
the A-side and is all the better for it. The line 'With extreme prejudice we're
gonna terminate our mission' is another reference to dialogue in the script of
the movie *Apocalypse Now.* (A different scene had already been referenced in

87

'Charlie Don't Surf' on *Sandinista!*). The Clash were to incorporate themes around the Vietnam War more fully in *Combat Rock*. The lyric 'Even angels wear their helmets on the morning of the 6th' is a reference to the dropping of the first atomic bomb on Hiroshima on 6 August 1945.

The artwork for the 7" single sleeve was designed by Futura 2000 who can be heard rapping on 'Overpowered by Funk' on *Combat Rock*.

'This Is Radio Clash' (12" EP – 1981)
Personnel:
Joe Strummer: vocals, guitar
Mick Jones: backing vocals, guitar
Paul Simonon: bass
Topper Headon: drums
Gary Barnacle: Saxophone
Ellen Foley: vocals
Produced by The Clash
UK release date: 4 December 1981.
US release date: 25 November 1981.

Side One
'This Is Radio Clash' / 'Radio Clash' (The Clash) Lead vocal – Joe
The Clash were well and truly working on a line of dance-orientated music after the success of 'The Magnificent Dance' and now started to release 12" singles and EP's back to back. Side One of the 12" EP contains the two tracks identical to the 7" single versions (above).

'This Is Radio Clash / Radio Clash' was performed at several concerts prior to its release, including when The Clash played in May/June at Bond's in Times Square, New York. The venue had been illegally oversold by the promoter, and so in order to honour the number of tickets sold The Clash volunteered to play 17 gigs instead of the 8 scheduled (for no additional financial gain to themselves). This brought the band a high profile with a lot of positive publicity, and although *Sandinista!* had contained no self-eulogising material, this was to change again with the release of 'This Is Radio Clash'. The 12" EP version was released on both sides of the Atlantic.

Side Two
'Outside Broadcast' / 'Radio 5' (The Clash) Lead vocal – Joe
The Clash are really kicking the arse out of 'Radio Clash' with these two tracks. 'Outside Broadcast' is a sort of messed-up dance mix. There are some vaguely amusing quips here and there like Joe's pidgin Spanish and his slowed-down vocal, but the lyrics are poor, and simply hearing Ellen Foley singing 'This Is Radio Clash' ad nauseam is enough to try the patience of even the most hardcore fan. 'Radio 5' is an unremarkable shorter, cacophonous dub version.

There Ain't No Asylum Here...

Combat Rock (LP – 1982)

Personnel:
Joe Strummer: vocals, guitar, percussion
Mick Jones: vocals, guitars, bass, piano, harmonica
Paul Simonon: vocals, bass
Topper Headon: drums, percussion, bass, piano
Additional contributors: Allen Ginsberg, Tymon Dogg, Tommy Mandell, Gary Barnacle, Futura 2000, Kosmo Vinyl, Ellen Foley, Joe Ely
Produced by The Clash and Glyn Johns
UK release date: 14 May 1982.
Highest position in UK chart; 2
US release date: 14 May 1982.
Highest position in US chart: 7

The weakest of the five Clash albums and paradoxically/predictably their most commercially successful, *Combat Rock* fulfilled its remit given by Bernie Rhodes that it should bring the band financial stability. With Rhodes back as manager (at Joe's insistence), he wanted commercial success to address the financial hole that The Clash had dug themselves, having released their previous two albums at generously low prices. Rhodes immediately saw that the obvious solution was for The Clash to release a single album, retailing at the regular price and containing a couple of hit singles. Joe wanted a clear direction of travel, and with Rhodes steering the boat this meant the exploitation of The Clash 'image' of uncompromising punk rock pioneers. Mick wanted to take the music in a new direction, but Rhodes was keen to manipulate the legacy to provide financial sustainability and/or to cynically cash-in on his own creation (depending on your point of view).

In April 1981 The Clash had started to record ideas of songs for the new album in Marcus Music Studio in London. They recorded 'This Is Radio Clash' and early versions of 'Sean Flynn' and 'Car Jamming'. After a series of live dates, recording sessions started again in August/September that same year in Ear Studios using The Rolling Stones' mobile recording facility, but tensions within the band were strained, with very little communication taking place. Here they recorded several new songs including 'Midnight To Stevens', 'First Night Back In London' and 'Long Time Jerk'. Mick was unhappy with the recordings and on his insistence, they relocated to Electric Lady Studios in New York between November and December 1981. By January 1982 the new album, provisionally titled *Rat Patrol From Fort Bragg* was beginning to take shape as a 15 track 67-minute opus, mixed by Mick and intended by him to be another Double-LP. When Mick presented it to the band Strummer and Rhodes said 'No' and an impasse was reached.

The band started a two-month tour of Australasia and the Far East during which they unsuccessfully attempted to mix the album on their days off. It was also during this tour when The Clash were in Thailand that Pennie Smith took the photographs for the album artwork. Smith knew the band well and later stated that it was in the course of this photoshoot that she saw the band dissolving before her eyes. Paul fell ill and was hospitalised for a number of weeks, but eventually, the band returned to London to work on the album again. They were exhausted after five intense years of non-stop touring and an exceptionally high output of recorded music.

Topper now had a serious heroin addiction which had almost precluded The Clash from playing in Japan. Although his drumming and overall musical contribution was largely unblemished, he was in his own words 'out of control' and extremely difficult to live with. Meanwhile, Mick was hardly on speaking terms with Joe and Paul and was discourteously late to almost every band session. Eventually, the decision was made to employ the respected producer Glyn Johns to oversee the editing and remixing of the new LP now re-titled *Combat Rock* by Joe.

Mick's musical prowess was counterbalanced by his prima-donna rock star behaviour, and the latter came back to bite him in the arse when the album was edited down. Glyn Johns and Joe had started work at 11am in the morning, so when Mick didn't turn up until 7.30pm the decision had already been made in his absence to cut the album down to a 47-minute long set of twelve tracks suitable for a single LP. Johns had culled the two 'left-field' tracks 'Kill Time' and 'The Beautiful People Are Ugly Too'. He had also culled 'First Night Back In London' and 'Cool Confusion' (both of which surfaced later as B-sides). After removing these from the album, Johns brought in 'Overpowered By Funk' which had hitherto kept separate from the album by Mick (probably with the intention of releasing it on a 12" single). Mick was unhappy, but in the end he went along with the decision. The ever-present fault lines in the band were now about to reach breaking point. Mick and Joe's perspectives were now diverging to such an extent that the songwriting partnership they had formed was beginning to visibly and audibly disintegrate.

Lyrically, the album continued and expanded on the post-Vietnam War theme, initially explored in 'Charlie Don't Surf' from *Sandinista!* The look of The Clash had changed very quickly over five years from punks with spiky hair in bespoke DIY clothes, through sleek rude boys and now quiff-sporting 'Urban Vietnam' veterans. The overall look of the band and the *Combat Rock* artwork do have a distinctive visual coherence which was to be of no small assistance in the marketing of the LP. The lyrics printed on the inner sleeve either by design or error include some (now absent) verses from the *Rat Patrol* versions.

Combat Rock was to become the swansong of one of the best rock 'n' roll bands of all time. Well packaged, with a couple of good singles, Combat Rock did indeed belatedly bring fiscal sustainability to The Clash – thereby simultaneously announcing the end of that same band as an alternative to the mainstream and as a counter-cultural entity. Commercial success was to undermine what the band were all about in the first place, but it was also becoming apparent that The Clash were anyway approaching the end of the road as a band.

Glyn Johns fulfilled his mandate and did a good job with some eclectic and underdeveloped material. His work on the two best songs 'Straight to Hell' and 'Rock The Casbah' is excellent; however *Combat Rock* is a strange album. It undoubtedly contains a few great songs and even more good ideas, but the mixed quality of the material is perhaps a clue that The Clash had run its course. John Lennon once said that The Beatles' *White Album* was the sound of that band breaking up. *Combat Rock* is the sound of The Clash breaking up.

Side One
'Know Your Rights' (Strummer/Jones) Lead vocal – Joe

'This is a pubic service announcement – With guitars!' Joe loved to include a lyrical introduction at the start of songs for The Clash (e.g. 'Version City'), and in his later work with The Mescaleros (e.g. 'Cool 'n' Out'). After the intro, the band kicks in with an abrasive Rockabilly groove as Topper and Paul drive the backing track under Mick's 1950s-style twangy guitars.

Written by Joe (who said that he based his lyric loosely on 'Ten Commandments' by Prince Buster), 'Know Your Rights' lacks the nuance and satirical sophistication of his earlier work and presents more like the prose of a petulant adolescent. His lead vocal (re-recorded by Johns) also lacks the implied humour of the version on *Rat Patrol*, and the overall sense of irony presumably intended by Joe somehow goes awry. The Clash had travelled a long way since the release of their first record, but the lyric for 'Know Your Rights' sounds like a clunky follow-up single to 'White Riot' with its simplistic street politics – but half a decade too late.

'Car Jamming' (Strummer/Jones/Simonon) Lead vocal – Joe

Combat Rock begins to gain traction with 'Car Jamming'. Topper kicks us off with a beat on the tom-toms that produces a primal rhythm for Mick and Paul to build an ascending chord sequence over the verses followed by a descending bass at the end of the chorus. Ellen Foley augments the backing vocal and the whole piece feels like The Clash moving towards interesting new musical territory.

Joe gives us a glimpse of his talent as a lyricist again in a stanza expressing empathy towards a Vietnam veteran draftee

> Then the shy boy from Missouri – Boots blown off in a '60s war
> Riding aluminium crutches
> Now he knows the welfare kindness – Agent Orange colour blindness
> As he works from door to door [24].

The fascinating lyric includes references to the inhabitants of the unforgiving concrete jungle where

> By ventilation units where towers meet the streets
> The ragged stand in bags soaking heat up through their feet.

91

At the end is an apparently random reference to Lauren Bacall – except to say that Mick did in fact see her walking her dogs in Westwood, Los Angeles one time. The Clash were in town having just played a local gig. Mick jokingly recalled how when she saw him, she did a 'double-take' because of his resemblance to Humphrey Bogart.

'Should I Stay Or Should I Go' (Strummer/Jones) Lead vocal – Mick

Possibly the most famous Clash song of all and entirely written by Mick, 'Should I Stay Or Should I Go' has a twelve-bar blues structure over a simple but instantly appealing melody (and is not unlike 'Little Latin Lupi Lu' by Bill Medley). A foot-stomping rhythm and wonderfully fat distorted bass drive the verses with guitars panned left and right. The choruses are played at double-time which gives them a frantic feel before the verse eases back into the original format with space for all sorts of shenanigans by the band.

With the benefit of hindsight, critics have labelled this as Mick pre-empting his dismissal from the band, but Mick is adamant that this was not the case. Scratch the surface and it becomes clear that this is simply another attempt by Mick to write a classic bubble-gum earworm. Only the fourth and definitely the last love song from The Clash, it lacks the gentle melancholy of 'The Street Parade' and the Soul sensibility of 'Train In Vain', but hits the mark on another agenda – that of a straight forward catchy pop song but beefed up by a terrific arrangement. It's an uncomplicated crowd-pleaser with all the hallmarks of a stadium-rock classic, serendipitously timed to coincide with The Clash's launch into bigger venues around the world.

The hard-rocking arrangement is given an upbeat boost by the backing vocals featuring both Joe Strummer and Joe Ely. Their mischievous enthusiasm is infectious, giving the whole track a light-hearted feel. Strummer had decided to sing in Spanish [25] but was unsure of the correct words, so he asked the engineer Eddie Garcia to phone his Ecuadorian mother to help compose the Spanish lyric. The result is a sort of nonsense Ecuadorian Spanish – but what the lyric lacks grammatically, it more than makes up for in fervour. The two Joes got under Mick's feet while he was laying down the lead vocal, and he told them both to 'Split!' This was kept and became part of the final mix.

'Rock The Casbah' (Strummer/Jones/Headon) Lead vocal – Joe

Topper had the music for this one kicking around for a while and so one day when he was at the recording studio on his own, waiting for the rest of the band to turn up, he just started recording it. He began by laying down the piano and drums, added the bass and then presented the result to the rest of the band who loved it. The original recording was shorter, consisting of only two verses and choruses, but it was simply spliced together and lengthened and then Joe wrote the bulk of the lyric almost immediately.

Bernie Rhodes had previously heard 'Sean Flynn' and had dismissively described it as a 'Raga'. Joe made a mental note and jotted down the line

'The King told the boogiemen / You have to let that raga drop' and this was to become the opening line of 'Rock The Casbah'. Joe had read an article about people in Iran being flogged for owning a disco record, and that became the inspiration for the lyric. 'Rock The Casbah' gently pokes fun at the oppressors who 'fundamentally can't take it' and look as ridiculous as they are frightening in trying to resist the appeal of popular music to the masses – not unlike Hitler's rejection of Jazz and Swing as 'Degenerate Negro music'.

'Rock the Casbah' was picked up on immediately by the Clash faithful and the general public alike as a great song. Topper's instantly likeable piano-based groove was boosted by an archetypal Joe Strummer lyric, which not only comments on an important geo-political issue, but also contains a distinctively humanitarian quality alongside his trademark humour – 'The Bedouin they brought out an electric camel drum'. The inclusion in the lyric of words like 'Minarets' and 'Muezzin' in particular bring to mind Joe's birthplace of Ankara and point to his intelligent and extensive vocabulary under his carefully cultivated 'everyman' image. Mick's input in musical terms was much less than usual on this particular track, but his wristwatch features as a sound effect during the third verse!

'Red Angel Dragnet' (Strummer/Simonon) Lead vocal – Paul

'Red Angel Dragnet' had started life as a poem by Joe about the contentious shooting of Frank Melvin, a member of the 'Guardian Angels' [26] on 29th December 1981 in New Jersey. The lyrics attempt to conflate this tragedy with the fictional Vietnam veteran turned vigilante Travis Bickle played by Robert De Niro in the in the seminal film by Martin Scorsese – *Taxi Driver* [27].

Paul's half-spoken, half monotone vocal sounds wooden and awkward, and the lyrics are very poor indeed. After expressing approval for the Guardian Angels, and what appears to be a reference to the Victorian murderer Jack The Ripper, the lyrics descend into incoherent babble. The song is interspersed with a monologue taken from *Taxi Driver*, unconvincingly recited by Kosmo Vinyl.

Musically, Topper's drumming is as competent as ever, and Paul sets the groove up with a relatively simple bassline and a jarring guitar sound, bringing to mind the discordant rhythm of a New York subway train.

'Red Angel Dragnet' might be viewed as a piece that attempts to join the dots between war veterans like Travis Bickle and the 'urban Vietnam' in New York City as depicted by Scorcese. In the final analysis, 'Red Angel Dragnet' is a poor song which ends up looking and sounding more like a fashion statement than the work of an important band.

'Straight To Hell' (The Clash) Lead vocal – Joe

The best track on Combat Rock by a mile and described by Joe as 'One of our absolute masterpieces', with 'Straight to Hell' The Clash take us into hitherto uncharted territory with a startlingly original musical ambience. Joe's lyrics glide effortlessly from a Britain undergoing de-industrialisation, through post-imperial Indochina and into drug addiction in 'Junkie-dom USA' in one seamless sweep with the ghost of the Vietnam War ever-present in the background.

Written and recorded in a last-minute flurry of artistic inspiration, the origins of 'Straight to Hell' were in a guitar riff Mick had been playing around with for a while. Aware that a rock beat was inappropriate, Topper gave Joe a lemonade bottle wrapped in a towel and asked him to beat the basic rhythm on the bass drum while he himself played a Bossa Nova pattern. Meanwhile Mick manipulates his guitar sound to create the distinctive oriental flavour, while Paul's bass brings coherence by holding the musical phrases together. This is the sound of The Clash pushing the boundaries and coming up with the goods.

The lyric begins by eloquently describing the effects of industrial decline in northern Britain on the lives of ordinary working people. In 1981 the Thatcher Government was closing down the heavy industries in the UK heartlands and the sense of desolation is expressed

As railhead towns feel the steel mills rust / Water froze in the generation
Clear as winter ice / This is your paradise.

The consequence was to condemn entire communities to the scrapheap of long-term unemployment 'There ain't no need for ya', with the only alternative being to join the military and be posted to a conflict in some God-forsaken corner of the globe 'Go straight to Hell, boys'.

Next, we are transported to the other side of the world to the cohort of Vietnamese children fathered by American soldiers during the war 'Wanna join in a chorus of the Amerasian blues?' The simple but haunting melody holds the listener's attention while subtly pointing out the human cost of conflict and social upheaval on the lives of the poor.

The anti-militarist theme of *Combat Rock* is explored beautifully, and although this song was recorded on the last day of 1981, it uncannily appears to have prophesised the Falklands War in the South Atlantic between The UK and Argentina that broke out only a few months later in April 1982.

It could be anywhere. Most likely could be any frontier – any hemisphere. [28]

On *Rat Patrol From Fort Bragg* 'Straight to Hell' is a wonderfully rambling work of just under seven minutes (which found its way onto both *The Clash On Broadway* and the *Sound System* compilations). For *Combat Rock* it was edited down to 5.31 by Glyn Johns who also significantly improved the production. In doing so, Johns has teased out the very best of The Clash during their most fractured period. 'Straight To Hell' lifts *Combat Rock* from a poor album (by Clash standards) to a patchy one which just happens to contain their magnum opus.

Side Two

'Overpowered By Funk' (Strummer/Jones/Headon) Lead vocal – Joe

The roots of 'Overpowered By Funk' may be detected in the musical diaspora of *Sandinista!* After the success of 'The Magnificent Dance' and 'This Is Radio Clash', Mick and Topper continue to mine the vein of dance tunes as they take a stab at penning an unapologetic Funk track [29]. The ironic lyric describes life as 'repetitive...asinine...stupefying', alluding to the similarities of the incessant rhythm of Funk, but also points out that as dance music, it's supposed to be visceral and escapist. In juxtaposing shallow consumerism 'Dog food...Breakfast Serials' (sic) with weighty issues of human tragedy 'Home for the floating people' [30] the lyric is holding the mirror up to society's 'Western ways'. Topper is clearly at home playing dance music, and Mick plays his variations on sus7 chords, but the sound doesn't quite swing. With no Norman Watt-Roy on hand to assist, the repetitive bass line feels slightly laboured and soulless.

The Clash used the platform to give Futura [31] a chance to flex his rapping muscles, but his words lack the intelligence and humour of Joe's work. The high-end slap-bass riff that appears just prior to Futura's appearance borrows heavily from a similar riff in 'This Is Radio Clash'.

Recorded over several sessions, and with Tommy Mandell playing keyboards (credited as Polly Mandell), the track does manage to capture the New York ambience of innovative contemporary bands like Talking Heads. 'Overpowered By Funk' may have worked better as the full-length 12" single dance track initially envisaged by Mick, but ends up sounding slightly incongruous, edited down and then shoehorned into the running order as the opening track on Side Two of a 'Rock' album.

'Atom Tan' (Strummer/Jones) Lead vocal – Joe/Mick

Based on a simple repetitive tune with a start/stop arrangement, 'Atom Tan' epitomises a frequent fault line running through much of *Combat Rock* in that it seems to present the kernel of an underdeveloped song rather than a coherent rounded piece. The phrase 'atom tan' brings to mind the image relating to 'Stop The World' on the rear of 'The Call Up' 7" single sleeve that illustrates the impact of an atomic explosion on the human form. The lyric also carries another theme later developed in 'Ghetto Defendant' – where seismic shifts on the geopolitical stage '...did not affect the steady sale of junk'. Drugs, alcohol and consumerism are different types of sedatives for the masses that divert attention from the actual underlying issues.

With genuine resistance failing to materialise, our narrator is forced to scan the horizon for a superhero to come and save the day. The disconnected, almost stream-of-consciousness lyric is shared between Joe and a multi-tracked Mick in a question/answer construction. The largely monotone chords under an unimaginative melody are given an element of colour by some bass movement under the chorus and Topper's stuttering percussion, but the generally weak music combined with the transparently superimposed, clumsy lyric make 'Atom Tan' one of the lesser tracks on *Combat Rock*.

'Sean Flynn' (The Clash) Lead vocal – Joe

Sean Flynn (the son of the actor Errol Flynn) was a photojournalist in Vietnam at the time of the war. He was captured in 1970 in Cambodia by the Viet Cong and was never seen again. He was probably murdered by The Khmer Rouge in

1971. The unnamed photojournalist played by Dennis Hopper in the movie *Apocalypse Now* is said to have been based on him.

The Clash song 'Sean Flynn' was one of the first songs to be recorded for *Combat Rock*. It was started in April 1981 in Marcus Music Studios, England when Mick began to create an ambient piece built around Topper's intriguing oriental soundscape. Exotic percussion stops and starts while flute and saxophone come in and out of focus as the listener is enticed into a trippy state of dreamy semi-consciousness. 'Sean Flynn' could be viewed as a partner to 'Straight to Hell', but at no point does it crystallise into the latter's coherence and is deliberately unfocused and an acquired taste.

The film *Apocalypse Now* explores the conflict between the light and darkness that reside in every human soul. In 'Sean Flynn', Joe places Flynn into the film's theme and uses this image to reflect every individual's personal journey through their own heart of darkness as 'each man knows what he's looking for'. The lyrics are less direct than usual and leave the listener to fill in the gaps. The music does the heavy lifting as an exceptionally evocative ambient piece with the atmosphere of sweaty, tropical claustrophobia.

Gary Barnacle played the saxophone during the original recording sessions, but his part became less prominent as the recorded track passed through its subsequent incarnations. The original seven and a half-minute version recorded at Marcus Music (and later released on *Sound System*) was famously described (disparagingly) as a 'Raga' by Bernie Rhodes who wanted a shorter track. Glyn Johns 'de-cluttered' the track, thereby improving the sound but he also removed 3 minutes from the running time (as instructed). The original full-length version of 'Sean Flynn' might perhaps have been more compatible in the more expansive context of a double album, but as with many tracks on *Combat Rock*, the overriding sense is one of a lack of focus and unfinished work.

The arrangement also incidentally owes a debt to the ambient introduction to Mickey Gallagher's composition 'Manic Depression' which had appeared on Ian Dury & The Blockheads' album *Laughter* a year earlier.

'Ghetto Defendant' (Strummer/Jones/Simonon) Lead vocal – Joe

In 'Ghetto Defendant' Joe voices his opposition to heroin as clearly as ever. He sees heroin addiction as the most insidious factor in debilitating the underclass into a life of powerless servitude. His condemnation of the use of hard drugs can be tracked right back to 'Deny' on the first album via similar sentiments expressed throughout the Clash's creative tenure. (The elephant in the room was Topper's alcoholism and worsening addiction to opiates). Nevertheless, Joe presses on, pointing out that

It is heroin pity / Not tear gas nor baton charge / That stops you taking the city.

Sitting mostly over a lazy reggae beat and with Topper defiantly coming up with the percussive goods, the rambling lyric connects the street politics of poverty and disempowerment to drug-induced escapism. For the most part, the staccato guitars keep away from the offbeat, giving more of a dub feel to the music, albeit without the commensurate sense of air and space.

The Clash had met Allen Ginsberg [32] in New York in 1981, and in a spill-over from the *Sandinista!* collective spirit, he was invited to contribute to the recording of *Combat Rock*. Ginsberg asked them to name some funk/punk dances (The Worm / Slam Dance) and then put them into his poem that interweaves with the main vocal by Joe.

After flirting with Clash-style street politics, Ginsberg eulogises the French poet Rimbaud who was in Paris just after the siege of 1871 when the Paris Commune had temporarily taken over the city (not 1873). He goes on to name-check several historical and Cold War proxy conflicts around the globe, in Central America and beyond before returning to the main theme – 'Kick junk / What else can the poor worker do?' When conducting interviews about the album, Joe would stress the anti-heroin message. Topper's wild hedonism was so at odds with the message, that with hindsight 'Ghetto Defendant' was one of the strongest indications that something was about to give. As a song and as a collaborative creative piece, it was and is successful, and consequently 'Ghetto Defendant' is one of the better tracks on *Combat Rock*.

'Inoculated City' (Strummer/Jones) Lead vocal – Mick
Continuing with the anti-militarist theme of *Combat Rock*, Mick goes through the chain of command from the soldier in the battlefield, all the way up to the political puppeteers at the top. 'Inoculated City' has the instant appeal of a Mick Jones tune, but is a Strummer/Jones composition. The part-muted guitar and bass underpin the simple syncopation of the melody in the verses. Outside the verses, the guitars play more sustained phrases to temporarily open up the sound and add harmony. The song possesses an unsophisticated charm and the repetitive nature of the melody and first verse lyric emphasise the cyclical patterns of history. Taking an overview of wars initiated by and for the benefit of the elite, (usually justified as some sort of noble undertaking in a unified common cause), Mick begs to differ, stating 'We are tired of the tune'.

As a precursor to the use of samples in his later work with BAD, Mick took the audio from a contemporary TV advertisement for a toilet cleaner *2,000 flushes* in order to make the point that wars are being waged to preserve the capitalist system of vacuous Western consumption. The chemical manufacturers 'Flushco Inc.' issued a public rebuttal pointing out that their product had nothing to do with militarism and threatened legal action. This led to the sample being removed from copies of the album in the mid-1980s. A legal settlement was later reached and the sample reappears on subsequent pressings of *Combat Rock*.

'Death Is A Star' (Strummer/Jones) Lead vocal – Joe
The Clash wrong-foot their audience one last time with 'Death Is A Star'. Joe wrote the lyric about the practice of going to the movies to watch murder and mortality for entertainment as a form of displaced catharsis. Good triumphs over evil on the cinema screen as an antidote the injustices of daily life

By chance or escaping from misery / By suddenness or in answer to pain
Smoking in the dark cinema / See the bad go down again

– a kind of modern equivalent to public executions as our collective nemesis
get their just desserts. Both Joe and Mick's vocals (panned hard to the sides)
are intimate and gentle and Joe half sings half speaks the piece while a scratchy
orchestration plays in the background. Enigmatic and haunting, with Tymon
Dogg on piano and Topper playing with brushes while a ukulele-style guitar plays
a simple strumming pattern, it feels cinematic, but simultaneously understated.
Intriguing – more like a question than an exclamation mark from one of the best
bands of all time, it doesn't offer any sort of resolution or closure but somehow
leaves the door open to possibility. The future is, after all, unwritten.

'Know Your Rights' (7" Single – 1982)
Personnel:
Joe Strummer: vocals, guitar
Mick Jones: guitar
Paul Simonon: bass
Topper Headon: drums
Produced by: The Clash / Glyn Johns
UK release date: 23 April 1982. Highest chart position in the UK: 43
US release date: N/A

A-side
'Know Your Rights' (Strummer/Jones) Lead vocal – Joe
Identical to album version (above)

B-side
'First Night Back In London' (Strummer/Jones/Simonon)Lead
vocal – Joe
With the exception of 'Mustapha Dance', all of the B-sides from the *Combat Rock*
singles were substandard. This one is about being stopped and searched by the
police in London who are looking for drugs but don't find them. The music has
a slightly threatening underworld feel with a few dodgy 1960s sci-fi sound effects
thrown in for good measure, but with a clunky melody and poor lyrics it's just not
a very good song. It was taken from the Ear Studio recordings from September
1981. With hindsight, this half-baked song can be seen as clear evidence that The
Clash were losing focus and were beginning to run out of road.

'Rock The Casbah' (7" Single – 1982)
Personnel:
Joe Strummer: vocals, guitar
Mick Jones: vocals, guitar
Paul Simonon: bass

Topper Headon: piano, bass, drums
Produced by: The Clash / Glyn Johns
UK release date: 11 June 1982.
Highest chart position in the UK: 30 (1982) / 15 (1991)
US release date: June 1982.
Highest chart position in the US: 8

A-side
'Rock The Casbah' (Strummer/Jones/Headon)Lead vocal – Joe
Remixed by Mick and Bob Clearmountain for the single, there are not too
many differences from the album version. The front cover of the picture sleeve
features Bernie Rhodes dressed as an Arab. Initial copies contained a sheet of
stickers and the song was also released as in the UK as a 7" picture disc.
Ironically the Don Letts promo video for the song features Terry Chimes
playing drums. Topper – the song's main author – had been thrown out of the
band a month before.

B-side
'Long Time Jerk' (Strummer/Jones/Simonon)Lead vocal – Joe
Another substandard B-side that was recorded at Ear Studios in September
1981 and a similarly poor offering to 'First Night Back In London', this time
featuring inferior quality, slightly soppy lyrics over an unimaginative melody.
The Cajun-influenced backing track shuffles along and the whole thing sounds
like a studio jam. This is not The Clash's finest moment.

'Rock The Casbah' (12" Single – 1982)
Personnel:
Joe Strummer: vocals, guitar
Mick Jones: vocals, guitar
Topper Headon: piano, bass, drums
Produced by: The Clash / Glyn Johns
UK release date: 18 June 1982.
US release date: 2 October 1982.

A-side
'Rock The Casbah' (Strummer/Jones/Headon) Lead vocal – Joe
Identical remix to the 7" single. There is more reverb added in places,
particularly on the third verse and the sound effects are slightly different.

B-side
'Mustapha Dance' (Strummer/Jones/Headon) Lead vocal – Joe
Just when it appeared that The Clash had lost the plot with a couple of shite
B-sides, this great dance version of 'Rock The Casbah' appears on the B-side
of the 12" single. 'Mustapha Dance' has Topper's fantastic bassline to the fore

and the lead vocal almost completely absent. Like the A-side, it was mixed by Bob Clearmountain at The Power Station in New York, but with Mick firmly in the producer's chair. This was to be the last of the dance-orientated 12" singles with Mick at the helm, and his last work in the studio with The Clash until he was involved in overseeing re-releases and re-mastering some decades later.

'Straight To Hell' / 'Should I Stay Or Should I Go' (7" Single – 1982)

Personnel:
Joe Strummer: vocals, guitar, percussion
Mick Jones: vocals, guitar
Paul Simonon: bass
Topper Headon: drums, percussion
Joe Ely: backing vocals
Produced by: The Clash / Glyn Johns
UK release date: 17 September 1982 / 1991.
Highest chart position: UK: 17 (1982) / 1 (1991)
US release date: 10 June 1982 [33].
Highest chart position US: 45

AA-side
'Straight To Hell' (The Clash) Lead vocal – Joe
On *Rat Patrol From Fort Bragg* 'Straight to Hell' is an opus of just under seven minutes. It was edited down to 5.31 by Glyn Johns for the *Combat Rock* album but was then desecrated into a 3.57 version for this release as a 7" single. Initial UK copies included a sticker where it was also released as a 7" picture disc.

A-side
'Should I Stay Or Should I Go' (Strummer/Jones) Lead vocal – Mick
Identical to album version (above)
Double A-side with 'Straight To Hell', but 'Should I Stay Or Should I Go' was immediately picked up by radio stations and was treated as the sole A-side. The video was filmed by Don Letts at the Shea Stadium and so features Terry Chimes on drums.

'Should I Stay Or Should I Go' was to become much more famous a decade later, reaching a mass audience following its use in a TV advert for Levi Jeans in 1991. This did open The Clash up for reasonable criticism as this could be construed as a clear example of 'turning rebellion into money'. Its use for the advert was Mick's decision and the rest of the band had given their blessing as they all regarded it as his song to do with as he pleased. It became The Clash's only number 1 single on its re-release in that same year, and had the positive effect of bringing The Clash's music to a wider audience. The 1991 re-release featured a song called 'Rush' on the B-side by Mick's new band, *Big Audio Dynamite*.

'Straight To Hell' / 'Should I Stay Or Should I Go' (12" Single – 1982)
Personnel:
Joe Strummer: vocals, guitar, percussion
Mick Jones: vocals, guitar
Paul Simonon: bass
Topper Headon: drums, percussion
Joe Ely: backing vocals
Produced by: The Clash / Glyn Johns
UK release date: 17 September 1982.
US release date: N/A

A bit of a pointless release really. The version of 'Straight to Hell' is a slightly edited one. Releasing a single with both A and B-sides on the album had been previously unthinkable for The Clash prior to the return of Rhodes. As with 'Rock The Casbah', the record company marketing ploy of encouraging fans to buy the same product again as picture discs (or repackaged with 'free' stickers) shows a departure from the previous Clash philosophy of not ripping them off. There was no real attempt at genuine value for money other than a 'free' stencil given away with the record.

AA-side
'Straight To Hell' (The Clash) Lead vocal – Joe
Almost identical to the album version but 16 seconds shorter for some inexplicable reason.

A-side
'Should I Stay Or Should I Go' (Strummer/Jones) Lead vocal – Mick
Identical to album version (above)

The End Of The Clash

After *Combat Rock* was completed and ready for release, The Clash's manager Bernie Rhodes started to worry about advance ticket sales for the forthcoming tour and decided to pull a publicity stunt. He told Joe to 'disappear' for a while and to keep his whereabouts a secret between the two of them. The rest of the band were not privy to the plan. Joe dutifully went 'missing' on 21 April 1982. 'Know Your Rights' was released two days later and the tour was cancelled. The rest of the band were deliberately kept in the dark by Bernie and they were not happy about it. Joe decided not to keep in touch with Bernie and dropped completely off grid which necessitated the latter dispatching Kosmo Vinyl to find him, which he did – in France – about one month later.

In the meantime, Topper's heroin addiction was not only a source of major embarrassment to the band and their message (see 'Ghetto Defendant'), but also made his continued involvement in any collective endeavour untenable. The quality of his performances were starting to diminish and he was becoming impossible to live and/or work with. He was sacked within a week of the release of *Combat Rock* on 14 May, just days after Joe's return. The band contacted Terry Chimes and he agreed to play drums for the imminent tour of The States. He was only given five days notice and it is a testament to Chimes' ability that he was able to stand in for Topper and perform to the standards he did. This was nevertheless a papering over the cracks as the slow and painful demise of The Clash was now underway.

The 'Down at the Casbah Club' tour of the USA began on 29th May and The Clash were simultaneously beginning to achieve commercial viability for the first time thanks to increased record sales there. Mick had always aspired to a career in music and was enjoying the success, but he was now seriously at odds with Bernie and his overbearing, Machiavellian approach to the management of the band. Meanwhile, Joe was trying to reconcile his 'rebel' persona with the fact that The Clash were now making money after all. He now sported a *Taxi Driver*-style Mohawk haircut and was in serious danger of becoming a punk caricature. After a European tour, followed by some dates in the USA, The Clash played Shea Stadium, New York on the 12th and 13th of October. They were supporting The Who [34] and the audience was 80,000 strong for each performance. This was a long way from The Clash philosophy of playing smaller venues for a better atmosphere. On one hand, playing Shea was a logical step to acquire success in the USA, thereby ensuring increased exposure to a wider audience for the music of The Clash (and a commensurate increase in financial return). On the other hand, it was a betrayal of what The Clash had always stood for, and the irony of wealthy rock stars playing 'Career Opportunities' to a mass audience wasn't lost on Paul and Joe. Terry Chimes had pointed out in the very early days that the dual aspirations of becoming one of the biggest bands in the world and staying 'hungry' through uncompromising integrity and self-imposed austerity are inevitably irreconcilable in the long run. As financially comfortable guitar-toting rock stars, The Clash were increasingly becoming the monster they set out to slay.

Terry Chimes left the band at the end of 1982, and after holding auditions early the next year, Pete Howard was appointed as their new drummer. In May 1983 The (new) Clash played the US festival in California. They received $500,000 for the appearance but still managed to piss just about everyone off, displaying an ungracious petulance towards both their hosts and the audience.

By the end of August 1983 internal disagreements had reached breaking point and (prompted by Bernie and Kosmo) Joe sacked Mick. Paul went along with Joe – as he almost always did. With Mick gone the indefinable symbiosis that produced such an exceptionally high standard of musical output was well and truly broken, never to be captured again. Topper's sacking had ripped the spine out of the band, but when Mick was thrown out, his contribution as one half of an outstanding songwriting partnership and as a performer, arranger and producer left with him.

It was Mick that had gradually taken over the production of The Clash's recordings. He had started as a covert understudy of Simon Humphreys on the first album, through an apprenticeship under Sandy Pearlman and then with Bill Price alongside him, to effectively produce *London Calling* and *Sandinista!* Production credited to 'The Clash' inevitably meant 'Mick Jones'. With Mick gone, the band was effectively finished. This was the end of The Clash.

Live Recordings (Official releases)

Joe used to say that whenever The Clash played live, he was so busy trying to prevent a riot that he couldn't concentrate on musicianship. Consequently, live performances were all about the energy and enthusiasm and he, therefore, believed that any such recordings wouldn't make much of a good listen. It's true that The Clash were so good live, and there was so much mayhem that it must indeed have been difficult staying just the right side of the line that divided furious passion from utter chaos.

It should also be remembered that the 'live' recordings of concerts officially released by most artists almost always contain studio overdubs to address mistakes and technical inadequacies. There were very few properly recorded Clash concerts anyway (particularly before 1978), and that which is 'officially' available tends to post-date Topper's departure in April 1982 – a critical omission in terms of performance. Joe once stated with hindsight that 'I don't think we played a good gig after Topper was fired'.

From Here To Eternity (1999)

This collection of live recordings spanning from 1978 to 1982 contains some absolute gems that capture the excitement and raw energy of a Clash concert and is an essential part of the story.

On this album, there is a disproportionately small amount of performance material predating the release of *Combat Rock*. Consequently, of the 17 tracks on this collection, only nine were recorded prior to the departure of Topper. Terry Chimes is a perfectly competent drummer, but the band simply does not have the same level of collective attack without Topper. In short, the tracks that feature Topper on drums are the best, so predictably the performances tail off a bit towards the end without him.

The early live performances like 'What's My Name' are great and well worth having. 'City Of The Dead' was recorded for inclusion in *Rude Boy* but did not make it to the final cut and does not feature in that movie. Thankfully this version was preserved and included in *From Here To Eternity*. The opening track, 'Complete Control' is fantastic and is taken from the soundtrack of the aborted Don Letts movie *The Clash On Broadway* as were 'Train In Vain' and 'Guns Of Brixton'.

The slightly pedestrian-sounding 'Career Opportunities' is from the second Shea Stadium gig and could well be included with a hint of irony. It also features a line about 'fighting in a Falklands street' referring to the armed conflict between Argentina and the UK earlier that year. (This version reappeared on *Live At Shea Stadium*).

'Capital Radio' is a particular highpoint with Joe's ad-lib outro fitting seamlessly into the performance. The different elements of the music are panned into a stereo image to reflect the band on stage (this was often the case with Clash records). Mick's guitar and vocals sit on the left and Paul's vocals are on the right. Mickey Gallagher's keyboards are panned slightly right to balance the sound, but in reality he was on Mick's side of the stage. 'Armagideon Time' features Mickey Gallagher again, along with additional toasting by Mikey Dread. The inclusion of these early recordings makes this the best live Clash collection.

Live At Shea Stadium (2008)

This album is a testament to the fact that The Clash were irrevocably damaged by the departure of Topper. On 13 October 1982, The Clash supported The Who at Shea Stadium for the second time in two days, playing to 80,000 people a night and this is the recording of that gig. The fact that it was recorded in a massive stadium rather than the more intimate venues that The Clash were used to is reflected in the fact that whole thing sounds a bit flat and uninspired. Clash publicist Kosmo Vinyl's somewhat stupid cockney caricature introduction is as irritating as it is contrived.

The whole album is a bit pointless in that it does not showcase a particularly remarkable performance and the absence of Topper doesn't help in this regard. It is a collection of excellent songs, professionally recorded and overdubbed, but simply does not represent The Clash at their peak. If you want to hear a better live recording of the Clash, start with *From Here To Eternity* and then check out some of the online footage or bootleg recordings made before 1982.

Not The Clash

Joe, having been manipulated into sacking Mick now felt the legacy and burden of The Clash sitting squarely on his shoulders. John Mellor had changed his name and his accent to don the persona of Joe Strummer, but he took a lot of demons along with him. Joe could be the kindest and most gracious host and a champion of the despised outsider. He could also be distant and offish to acquaintances and strangers alike and was perfectly capable of being ruthless and cruel for no apparent reason. He became a father in November 1983, had bought a house and employed a cleaner. The punk rock rebel had morphed into a 30-something, property-owning parent. These contradictions were the inevitable consequence of success and maturity, but they clearly troubled Joe who pressed on with Paul to what they thought at the time was the next logical step. They decided to get in two new guitarists so that Joe could concentrate on being the 'Front Man'. By December they had Nick Sheppard and Vince White [35] in the band.

They toured the USA and Europe in 1984, but it was never anything but a Clash tribute band. Joe's father died just before the spring and Joe's personal disorientation and isolation – exacerbated by Bernie Rhodes' management techniques – became even worse. The treatment of the new members – Pete, Nick and Vince was shoddy. In Vince's words, they were 'slaves to The Clash machine' and were underpaid and belittled by Bernie. In addition to the loss of his father, Joe was now dealing with the terminal illness of his mother and his mental health was clearly suffering. The unhappy ship was just about managing to keep afloat, but harsh reality kicked in when at the end of the year CBS were knocking on the door demanding another album. This was the point when Bernie's arrogance and manipulative behaviour started to outdo even that of his friend, Malcolm McLaren.

Rhodes booked a cheap studio in Munich to make the next 'Clash' album. Paul was away (not for the first time) during the recording of the new album, so Norman Watt-Roy was employed to play bass. Vince was sidelined and Pete Howard was substituted on the album by a drum machine. Joe displayed very little interest in the project. He failed to turn up to rehearsals and walked out of the recording sessions after only laying down mostly guide vocal tracks. He went off to find Mick Jones, finally tracking him down in The Bahamas and asked him to come back but Mick declined. His new band, Big Audio Dynamite (BAD) was starting to come together. Joe and Mick parted as friends.

Bernie relished the free hand he now had with the legacy of The Clash. He helped himself to 50% of the songwriting credits, produced a shit album, re-named it Cut The Crap and released it in November 1985 as if it was The Clash. Joe immediately disassociated himself from the album and then quit the band. Bernie then unashamedly tried to persuade Paul to carry on as 'The Clash' Front Man with Pete, Nick and Vince as his backing band. Paul refused and quit. Astonishingly Bernie then tried to carry on without Paul either, but in the end, was forced to concede that it was over. Bernie Rhodes was midwife to one of the greatest bands of all time. Unfortunately, he will mainly be remembered for rummaging through the pockets of the cold carcass of the only band that mattered.

Cut The Crap (LP) 1985

The personnel invoved in *Cut The Crap* are not listed. This is partly because the precise details of the recording and production are contentious. The main reason, however, is because the author refuses to validate the album as a legitimate release from The Clash.

Don't be conned into buying this album – It is not a Clash album and it is fucking awful. Some critics have said that under the veneer of Bernie Rhodes' piss-poor arrangement and production that there are some decent songs on *Cut The Crap*. There are not – they are all bad. The following songs are reviewed solely to ensure that this book is comprehensive.

Joe only recorded guide vocal tracks for *Cut The Crap*. He knew that the game was up and walked out at an early stage which left Bernie Rhodes to 'co-write', 'arrange' and 'produce' the album. There are some partially-formed half-ideas, but the football chants, crappy drum machines, shitty synthesisers and distorted guitars can't disguise the fact that the low-quality content of this album makes a mockery of The Clash's name. There is no humour and very little sophistication to the lyrics. In fact, there's even a song titled 'We Are The Clash' by a band that is clearly NOT The Clash. The music sounds like 1980s synth-pop of the lowest grade. What a load of shit this album is. With the possible exceptions of 'This Is England' and 'North And South' there is nothing of value on this album and no self-respecting Clash fan will own it. It is a pimple on the arse-end of The Clash.

'Dictator' (Strummer/Rhodes)
When the dreadful lyric of 'Dictator' is compared to something as fine as 'Washington Bullets', it's staggering that they both came from the hand of Joe Strummer. His talent as a lyricist is completely absent (as is the case for pretty much the whole album) and the lyrics are astonishingly clumsy. As for the music, there is no discernable melody in the verses and the chorus is poor. The production and instrumentation are laughably incompetent as painfully illustrated by the senseless audio samples and the intrusive cacophony of the tuneless synthesiser. It sounds like a toddler playing with a keyboard with the radio left on in the corner of the room. This track is a piece of shit and as such, sets the tone for the whole album.

'Dirty Punk' (Strummer/Rhodes)
Like the cover of the album, this track is a charmless caricature of punk rock. The tune is rubbish and the lyric is awful; 'Gonna be a dirty punk…Used to be the local hunk'. Embarrassing.

'We Are The Clash' (Strummer/Rhodes)
Immediately after Mick Jones was sacked in 1983, he got together with Topper for a short period and mischievously started ringing promoters stating that he would be using The Clash's name for his new project. This clearly put the wind up Joe

and Bernie, and so this song was written. It is the musical equivalent of a dog pissing on a lamppost. As for the song itself – It's shit (somewhat predictably). 'We ain't gonna be treated like trash…We are The Clash'. Bollocks you are.

'Are You Red..y' (Strummer/Rhodes)
This one starts with guitars but morphs into a dodgy 1980s synth-pop fest. The lyric is – you guessed it – clumsy, charmless and poor.

'Cool Under Heat' (Strummer/Rhodes)
This album just doesn't get any better. Another shit lyric superimposed on a tuneless backing track. OK – so there are not so many annoying synthesisers on show, but in the sections where the guitars aren't over-distorted the whole thing sounds like a soulless studio jam. Not good.

'Movers And Shakers' (Strummer/Rhodes)
The sentiment expressed in 'Career Opportunities' and 'All The Young Punks' seems to have been rubbished in 'Movers And Shakers'. It appears as if Joe was attempting a Springsteen-esque validation of the daily toil of the humble worker, scraping an honest living at the bottom of society, but the lyric is totally devoid of subtlety or eloquence. There is not much of a melody in the verses and the poppy chorus is poor. More synth-pop / football chant nonsense.

'This Is England' (Strummer/Rhodes)
The one half-decent song on *Cut The Crap* – badly recorded, produced and arranged – but certainly the pick of the bunch. Joe once described it as the 'last great Clash song', but the petulant lyrics in the verses are particularly poor, containing punk caricatures and half-cocked references to violence (state-sponsored and otherwise). The basic melody sounds like an outtake from Joe's below-par solo material, but this is anyway suffocated by Rhodes' incompetent interference in the music. The catchy chorus is better, but overall the song is substandard.

'This Is England' has been (graciously?) included in some posthumous Clash compilations including the singles box set and the anthemic refrain of the song title was used by Shane Meadows for his award-winning film set in Northern England in 1983.

'Three Card Trick' (Strummer/Rhodes)
Rhodes' poor production gets in the way of what initially appears to be a reasonably pleasant Ska-influenced arrangement, however, scratch the surface and 'Three Card Trick' is just another sub-standard, vacuous nothing of a song.

'Play To Win' (Strummer/Rhodes)
The closest to charm that this 'experimental' track gets is where Joe alludes to his love of cowboys. However, as an ambient piece 'Play to Win' fails where 'If

Music Could Talk' succeeded. The latter had Mikey Dread in the producer's chair and this one has Bernie Rhodes. Enough said.

'Fingerpoppin'' (Strummer/Rhodes)
Whereas Joe's vocal on 'This Is England' has some authenticity, this is now completely absent as this album reverts to type, Shit lyrics, shit song.

'North And South' (Strummer/Rhodes)
Sitting just below 'This Is England', this is possibly the only other track on *Cut The Crap* of any interest. Nick Sheppard takes the lead vocal for this one. In 1984, Britain was in the middle of The Miner's Strike, which ended up as a seminal moment in the social history of the UK. The North/South divide has roots going back over 1,000 years and Joe's sympathy for the communities affected by de-industrialisation was eloquently expressed in 'Straight To Hell'. 'North And South' is, by comparison very poor indeed, however in the context of *Cut The Crap* it is the closest to valid social comment that the album manages to achieve. The arrangement is not as poor as that on most of the tracks on *Cut The Crap*, and it does possess some kind of discernable melody. Overall, a poor song – just not as poor as the rest of the album.

'Life Is Wild' (Strummer/Rhodes)
Another shit song, indicative of the whole album. Bad lyrics, bad melody, badly produced and completely charmless.

'Do It Now' (Strummer/Rhodes)
Non-album track, released on the B-side of 'This Is England', this Ska-influenced song is of a similarly low quality to the tracks on the album albeit with less interference from Rhodes. The track has an upbeat feel, but seems to compare hostility towards punks to that of racism experienced by the Windrush generation. I don't think so, Joe.

'Sex Mad Roar' (Strummer/Rhodes)
Additional track on the B-side of the 12" of 'This Is England', many fans were mystified why this track wasn't on the album, given that it was one of the better new songs played live by 'The Pantomime Clash'. A Rockabilly workout which was originally titled 'Sex Mad War'. Possibly an anti-pornography song, but still nowhere near the standards of The Clash proper.

Compilations
'The Clash' (LP – US Version) (1979)
Joe had been scathing of the American corporate executives who were the
targets of his boredom with the USA (and not the American people who he
described as "well ahead" of the music industry there). Epic (CBS) didn't
release The Clash's first album in The United States until after *Give 'em Enough
Rope*, decreeing that it was technically inadequate and therefore not suitable
for the American market. Meanwhile, the UK version of the first album sold
100,000 copies in America as an import, and when Epic did eventually release
it there, they changed the track listing – removing four of the original songs
('Deny', 'Cheat', 'Protex Blue' and '48 Hours') and mainly replacing them with
the A-sides of The Clash's early British singles. 'Gates of the West' and 'Groovy
Times' also found their way into that same release as a limited edition 7" single
given away free with the LP.

'Black Market Clash' (10" Mini-LP 1980)
This was a mini-LP released in the USA at the back end of 1980 to allow fans
there to augment their collection of Clash songs with tracks that had hitherto
been unavailable in the States. The collection also contained two tracks that
were at that time unavailable in the UK, so the album sold as an import until
released there domestically in 1983. It is the only compilation to have appeared
whilst the band were still together. The iconic front cover photograph shows
Clash friend and co-conspirator Don Letts at The Notting Hill Carnival in 1976.
The tracklisting was as follows;

Side One
1. 'Capital Radio One' (Strummer/Jones)
Identical version to that on the *Capital Radio EP* (1977). It has been re-named
here to distinguish it from the second version of the same song that had been
recorded for *The Cost of Living EP* in 1979.

2. 'The Prisoner' (Strummer/Jones)
B-side to '(White Man) In Hammersmith Palais' 7" single.

3. 'Pressure Drop' (F. Hibbert)
The recording that appeared on the B-side to 'English Civil War' 7" single was
remixed by Bill Price for inclusion on *Black Market Clash*. This remix includes
saxophone played by Gary Barnacle.

4. 'Cheat' (Strummer/Jones)
Album track from the UK original version of *The Clash* LP that had been deleted
from the US release of that same name.

5. 'City Of The Dead' (Strummer/Jones)
B-side to 'Complete Control' 7" single.

6. 'Time Is Tight' (Booker T. Jones)
Used by the band as a 'warm-up' song and originally by Booker T. and the MG's, this instrumental cover was recorded in March 1978 at Marquee Studios London. It features Gary Barnacle on saxophone and Steve Nieve on keyboards. The latter was returning the favour for Mick Jones who had played guitar on the Elvis Costello & The Attractions track 'Big Tears' a few months earlier. 'Time Is Tight' was mothballed and unused until it was dusted off and remixed by Bill Price in 1980 for inclusion on *Black Market Clash*. This track was not previously available in the UK.

Side Two
1. 'Bankrobber / Robber Dub' (Strummer/Jones/Campbell)
The full-length version of 'Robber Dub' was originally intended as a B-Side to a 12" single release of 'Bankrobber' as a dub version of that tune. When CBS declined to release 'Bankrobber' as a single, 'Robber Dub' was shelved. It was later edited down and spliced on to the end of 'Bankrobber' for *Black Market Clash* as one of the two tracks on the mini-LP not previously available. In the 'Robber Dub' section, Mikey Dread works his magic, boosting the bass and moving Joe's vocal in and out of earshot.

2. 'Armagideon Time' (Williams/Mittoo)
Double A-Side of 'London Calling' 7" single.

3. 'Justice Tonight / Kick It Over' (Williams/Mittoo)
An edited version of Side Two of 'London Calling' 12" EP.

'The Story Of The Clash Vol. 1' (1988)
A collection of single A-sides, EP and album tracks from 1977-1982. It consists of most of the well known songs and works as a whistle-stop tour of the band's music in lieu of a 'Greatest Hits' compilation. (That wouldn't work for The Clash anyway because they didn't have too many 'hits' as such). No Volume 2 exists.

'1977 Revisited' (1990)
This collection was compiled to fill in a US audience on the Clash songs they had missed out on due to most of the early releases being unavailable there. It is designed to sit alongside the US version of *The Clash* (1st LP) and *Black Market Clash* to cover all the non-album releases plus the four tracks omitted from the US version of *The Clash*. The only outstanding omissions would have been the UK LP version of 'White Riot' and the 1979 *Cost Of Living EP* version of 'Capital Radio'. Otherwise this more or less completes the collection for US fans up to and including the *London Calling* album.

'The Singles' (1991)
Simply a collection of the A-sides of all of The Clash's singles released in the UK in chronological order (plus 'Train In Vain' which sold in the UK as an import – see 'Bankrobber'). Not a bad place to start to explore the rest of The Clash's canon once you have the five studio albums.

'The Clash On Broadway' Box Set (1991)
While they were together, The Clash had steered clear of releasing compilation albums (*Black Market Clash* not withstanding), and were all about value for money. They generally managed to hold the line and stand against the record company standard rip-off of releasing an expensive collection of previously released material with a couple of 'newly available' songs. They let themselves down with *The Clash On Broadway* which largely contains tracks that were already available on albums or singles. The previously unreleased material comprises three sub-standard outtakes ('One Emotion', 'Every Little Bit Hurts' and 'Midnight To Stevens'), some edits and remixes from *Combat Rock*, a couple of the songs from *The Polydor Demos* and three live recordings. In order to get hold of these, diehard fans had to shell-out for a triple album box set of material, the majority of which they probably already had. The compilation was overseen by Kosmo Vinyl and was initially intended for the US market, but was made available in the UK to cash in on the recent success of the re-released 'Should I Stay Or Should I Go' and 'Rock The Casbah'.

The live versions of 'English Civil War' and 'I Fought The Law' were later remastered and released again on *Sound System*. The live version of 'Lightning Strikes' was recorded Bond's in New York on 9th June 1981 and is of mild interest, but unremarkable. The gig itself was part of the band's seventeen-gig marathon residency at the venue which was filmed by Don Letts with the intention of making a movie titled *The Clash On Broadway* (hence the song's inclusion). Most of the movie footage was lost – thought to have been destroyed. Some of the surviving footage was included in the 'This Is Radio Clash' video.

'One Emotion' (Strummer/Jones) Lead vocal – Mick/Joe
Recorded at Basing Street during the *Give 'em Enough Rope* sessions, the title 'One Emotion' was originally a piss-take of the actor Roger Moore, playing the part of James Bond. Joe is audibly trying to develop a scat a lyric to make it into a coherent song, but doesn't quite pull it off, hence the track's exclusion from previous Clash releases.

'Every Little Bit Hurts' (Cobb) Lead vocal – Mick
This is a cover of the Brenda Holloway Motown classic, originally written by Ed Cobb. Mick used to sing it with Chrissie Hynde when they were friends in the early days. She visited him during the *Sandinista!* sessions and so Mick got the idea to record it. The accompanying arrangement is perfectly competent, but unfortunately Mick does not really possess the vocal capacity

to deliver a truly soulful rendition. Nevertheless, it is impossible not to enjoy hearing the song itself.

'Midnight To Stevens' (Strummer/Jones) Lead vocal – Joe
Recorded in September 1981 using The Rolling Stones' mobile studio at Ear Studios, London, 'Midnight To Stevens' was written for the producer Guy Stevens a few weeks after his death in August 1981. The first verse is Joe recounting his own semi-mythical odyssey, trawling through the pubs and bars of London in 1979 to locate Stevens. When he finally found him slumped over the bar, Joe persuaded Stevens to produce the album that would become *London Calling*. The song has a melancholy ambience, relying heavily on a simple prominent lead guitar riff but doesn't really go anywhere and the lyric is not up to Joe's usual high standards. 'Midnight To Stevens' is an interesting outlier but not an essential addition to a Clash collection.

'Super Black Market Clash' (1993)
A substantially expanded version of *Black Market Clash*, this compilation is quite extensive and sits nicely next to *The Singles* album to almost complete the works of The Clash alongside the five studio albums. It inexplicably misses out 'Armagideon Time' and the original version of 'Capital Radio' (both of these can be found on *Black Market Clash*). The version of 'Capital Radio' on *Super Black Market Clash* is titled 'Capital Radio Two' and is the 1979 version from *The Cost Of Living EP*.

Available for the first time is the full version of 'Listen'. Up until its inclusion on this compilation, only an edited version had been released on the original *Capital Radio EP*, released in 1977.

Also available here for the first time is the full version of 'Robber Dub' originally intended for inclusion on the 12" single of 'Bankrobber'. The 12" single was never released, but part of 'Robber Dub' was tacked onto the end of 'Bankrobber' and released on *Black Market Clash* as 'Bankrobber / Robber Dub'.

Also included is 'Cool Confusion' from the original *Rat Patrol From Fort Bragg* sessions which had only seen release in the US as a B-side and had been hitherto unavailable in the UK. The version of 'Long Time Jerk' on *Super Black Market Clash* is an edit lasting 2.57. The original was 5.08 in duration.

'The Essential Clash' (2003)
A 'Best of'-type compilation, made up of singles and album tracks put together as part of a record company 'Essential' series. It's not bad value for money and suitable for a novice, but clearly non-essential duplication for true Clash fans.

'London Calling – 25th Anniversary Edition' (2004)
This release comprises the original double-LP on one CD, plus a copy of *The Vanilla Tapes* (see 'rarities' below) and a bonus DVD which contains *The Last Testament* (a short documentary about the making of *London Calling*). Also on the DVD are the promo video for the single 'London Calling' and excellent live

performances of 'Train In Vain' and 'Clampdown' (both from The Lewisham Odeon, London on 18 February 1980), plus some footage of the band recording in Wessex Studio with Guy Stevens.

'The Singles' Box Set (2006)

A complete set of the UK singles by The Clash on 19 CDs or the same number of 7" vinyl records. Very nearly comprehensive, although somewhat inexplicably it does not include the reprise of 'I Fought The Law' (also called 'The Cost Of Living Advert') after 'Capital Radio' on *The Cost Of Living EP*. It does include 'This Is England' (see above).

'The Singles' (2007)

Contains the singles as per the 1991 version but also includes 'This Is England' from *Cut The Crap*. It does not include 'Train In Vain'.

'The Albums' – Re-mastered (2013)

The five studio albums re-mastered and nicely presented. An excellent place to start your Clash collection from scratch.

'Sound System' (Box set) (2013)

This very nicely packaged collection contains very nearly all of The Clash's recorded work including all five studio albums and all the singles, B-sides and EPs. The collection has benefitted from having been re-mastered by Mick. *Sound System* contains 12" mixes and extra audio recordings previously officially unavailable (such as unedited versions and outtakes from *Rat Patrol From Fort Bragg*). It also includes *The Beaconsfield Recordings*, *The Polydor Demos* and some live recordings.

In addition to the audio content above, there is a DVD included which contains some short films, interviews, promo videos and live footage. The packaging also includes fanzine facsimiles, stickers, badges and other goodies for the Clash obsessive.

Unfortunately, there are no lyric sheets for any of the non-album material. Neither is the *Sound System* collection exhaustive because it doesn't include 'Mustapha Dance', 'Justice Tonight / Kick It Over', 'The Cost Of Living Advert' or the full version of 'Robber Dub' (all of which are essential). Nor does it include 'One Emotion', 'Every Little Bit Hurts', the full version of 'Listen' or 'Radio 5' and 'Outside Broadcast' from the 'Radio Clash' 12" EP (none of which are essential). The *Capital Radio EP* 'Interview' is an edited version.

The audio 'Extras' 3 x CD set comprises the following tracks – all re-mastered by Mick Jones;

CD1

A very nearly complete collection of Singles, B-sides and EP tracks from 'White Riot' through to 'Bankrobber'.

CD2

1. '(The) Magnificent Dance' – from the B-side of the 12" single version of 'The Magnificent Seven'.
2. 'Midnight To Stevens' – from the early *Combat Rock* recording sessions. Previously released on *The Clash On Broadway*.
3. 'Radio One' – A shorter version than the one on the B-side of 'Hitsville UK'.
4. 'Stop The World' – B-side to 'The Call Up'.
5. 'The Cool Out' – An excellent instrumental version of 'The Call Up' remixed by 'Pepe Unidos' (i.e. Joe, Paul and Bernie) and with some added percussion. This track had not previously been released in the UK but had seen release in Europe and the USA on *The Magnificent Seven 12" EP*.
6/7. 'This Is Radio Clash' / 'Radio Clash' – A and B-sides of the 7" single.
8. 'First Night Back In London' – B-side to 'Know Your Rights'.
9. 'Rock The Casbah' – 12" single mix.
10. 'Long Time Jerk' – B-side to 'Rock The Casbah' 7" single.
11. 'The Beautiful People Are Ugly Too' – An outtake from *Rat Patrol From Fort Bragg*.
12. 'Idle In Kangaroo Court' – Alternative title 'Kill Time'. An outtake from *Rat Patrol From Fort Bragg*.
13. 'Ghetto Defendant' – Extended version from *Rat Patrol From Fort Bragg* with additional lyrics which were probably by Allen Ginsberg – although he is not credited as a co-author.
14. 'Cool Confusion' – An outtake from *Rat Patrol From Fort Bragg*, originally released in the US as the B-side to 'Should I Stay Or Should I Go'.
15. 'Sean Flynn' – Extended version from *Rat Patrol From Fort Bragg*. The original version was recorded at 'Marcus Music Studios' and features more extensive instrumentation and more prominent saxophone by Gary Barnacle.
16. 'Straight To Hell' – Extended version from *Rat Patrol From Fort Bragg*. Includes additional lyrics.

CD3

The third CD contains *The Polydor Demos*, four songs from *The Beaconsfield Recordings* and six live recordings from The Clash live at The Lyceum in London dated 28 December 1978 (although it appears they were in fact recorded at The Lyceum on 3 January 1979). Two of these recordings ('City Of The Dead' and 'I Fought The Law') had previously been available on *From Here To Eternity*.

'The Clash Hits Back' (2013)

Another sort of 'Best of' album released in the same year as the re-mastered albums and *Sound System*. The sequence was chosen to be close to the set played at The Brixton Fair Deal on 10 July 1982.

Selected Rarities

'The Polydor Demos' (1976)

The Clash made this demo in Polydor Studios in November 1976 and almost signed to Polydor Records a few weeks later, just before they were snapped up by CBS. This demo comprises five early Clash songs – 'Career Opportunities', 'White Riot', 'Janie Jones', 'London's Burning' and '1977'. Bernie Rhodes brought in his friend, Guy Stevens, to produce the recording. Stevens had worked with Mick's favourite band Mott The Hoople, and he would later produce the epic *London Calling* album, but *The Polydor Demos* are hugely disappointing by comparison. Stevens was going through a rough period in his personal life (and his relationship to alcohol) and so he simply wasn't up to the job at that time. Joe was encouraged by the engineer to sacrifice passion and immediacy for clear diction and the result is an unsatisfactory, bland rendition of some great songs. Joe is clearly not playing to his strengths in the vocal delivery. He hated the recording, describing it as 'Flat' and 'Boring'. Terry Chimes left The Clash after this recording. Neither the excitement nor the energy of the band is truly captured here which is why The Clash reverted to using their live sound engineer, Mickey Foote to produce their first album. *The Polydor Demos* do not capture any performances of particular quality and are thus of only passing interest to anyone other than Clash completists. All five tracks are included in the *Sound System* box set.

'The Beaconsfield Recordings' (1976)

This is the second studio recording of The Clash and it's definitely worth hearing. The performances are much better than *The Polydor Demos* which they postdate by a month or so.

Once the band had returned from the 'Anarchy' tour in late December 1976, they sneaked into Beaconsfield Film School in Buckinghamshire where their friend, Julien Temple was a student. He had a copy of the key to the camera room, so without permission, they just went in, recorded their music on an 8-track tape machine and made a short film. Some of the audio recordings and film footage are in the *Sound System* collection. Rob Harper had played drums for the 'Anarchy' tour, but he had just quit, so Terry Chimes agreed to help out at Beaconsfield, although he was deliberately kept out of camera shot for the film.

'I'm So Bored With The USA' is an interesting early version with the lyrics only half-finished. The Beaconsfield recording of 'White Riot' ended up on the first album (*The Clash*) after it was remixed the following year by Simon Humphreys. The other songs recorded at Beaconsfield were 'London's Burning', 'Janie Jones', 'Career Opportunities' and '1977'.

'The Vanilla Tapes' (1979)

After The Clash had returned to England from touring the US in early February 1979, they had sacked their manager (Bernie Rhodes) and consequently had no place to rehearse. They were deeply in debt to the record company and the British music press had turned on them. As one of the few survivors of the punk explosion, they had enemies on all sides and the vultures were beginning to circle.

Having shut themselves away in Vanilla Rehearsal Studios, they spent the summer writing and rehearsing new material. They decided to record what they had done and so they sent one of the crew out to buy some small, cheap, highly portable recording equipment. This was done and recordings were made of the rehearsals. Joe was keen to release these very basic recordings as an album in order to keep the production costs down so that the LP could be released at a very low price.

Eventually, the decision was made not to release the recordings in this way, but to send them to Guy Stevens and ask him to produce the album. A master copy was made of *The Vanilla Tapes*, but this was lost by a roadie (Johnny Green) who accidentally left it on a train seat. Another copy was made and this one was received by Stevens. *London Calling* was recorded at Wessex Studios and the original demo recordings themselves were thought to have been discarded (Stevens did not appear to keep his copy) and so *The Vanilla Tapes* were now presumed to have been irretrievably lost.

Then a copy of the tapes was discovered by Mick in 2004 and was subsequently released as a bonus disc with the *25th Anniversary Edition of London Calling*. The original tapes contained 37 tracks but there were several versions of the same songs, so it was reduced down to the 21 best versions that appear on the disc. There are three Clash original *London Calling* songs that did not appear on *The Vanilla Tapes*, namely 'Spanish Bombs', 'The Card Cheat' and 'Train In Vain', indicating that they were written later in the process of recording at Wessex. 'Wrong 'em Boyo' is also absent from the original tapes.

'Hateful' – A nice sharp take of an extended jam of the song with no vocal. Mick plays lead guitar, riffing on the melody.

'Rudie Can't Fail' – Joe and Mick's guitars are panned left and right respectively as a perfect illustration of their complementary styles. (This was the basic stereo layout for most Clash records). The lyric is incomplete and as with the rest of the session, the vocals are muffled, but the bare bones of this classic are nicely laid out and a pleasure to hear.

'Paul's Tune' – After an initial struggle with the tempo, this early draft of 'Guns Of Brixton' without vocals is built around the bassline. As the take progresses, the rest of the band can be heard feeling their way into the groove.

'I'm Not Down' – Topper's drumming really holds this one together, making it sound the most complete song so far with different lyrics, mainly in the verses.

'Four Horsemen' – Joe and Mick's guitars are panned left and right again, and the bass is inaudible on this track, but otherwise it's relatively complete with a more or less full lyric.

'Koka Kola, Advertising & Cocaine' – Paul counts in and after a false start, Joe leads the band through a couple of part-written verses and a chorus. The rest of the lyric is unwritten from the middle 8 to the end.

'Death Or Glory' – Essentially complete with some nice lead guitar work by Mick.

'Lover's Rock' – Again, essentially complete, this guitar chord heavy demo includes some harmonica, but most clearly illustrates how much the piano part brought to the final arrangement.

'Lonesome Me' – The Clash do Johnny Cash and the Cowboy Blues. It sounds like the boys from Blighty have just got back from The States – and they had. This one is credited to 'The Clash' but has the hallmark of a Mick Jones composition from the simple lyric, its subject matter, all the way through to his lead vocal. It's a bit cheesy, but it's also only an outtake.

'The Police Walked In 4 Jazz' – Acoustic and electric guitars are panned left and right respectively in this instrumental precursor to 'Jimmy Jazz'. There is some walking bass at the end but Paul generally sticks to the root note. Topper sounds well and truly in his element and there appears to be a (Small Faces-style) snippet of a studio jam tacked on to the end of the track.

'Lost In The Supermarket' – Mick double-tracks the lead vocal while the guitars are panned hard right and left. The composition sounds complete and awaiting a final performance and arrangement.

'Up Toon' – This instrumental backing track to 'The Right Profile' (lyric, as yet unwritten) has the air of strutting through the centre of town with your head held high. (The title may also be a pun, referring to the repeated key shifts). Apparently there was also an alternative version named 'Canalside Walk' recorded in the same sessions.

'Walking The Slidewalk' – Instrumental companion piece to 'Up Toon', but this time it's a jam built on a 12-bar blues structure. Joe's rhythm plays the offbeat while the lead and bass guitars play the melody with Mick going off on the occasional tangent.

'Where You Gonna Go (Soweto)' – Although credited to 'The Clash', this reggae jam is based on 'Fire In Soweto' by Sonny Okosun with Joe ad-libbing a vocal over the top.

'The Man In Me' – A Vanilla Studio quasi-jam wherein The Clash try their hand at a Bob Dylan song, working back from the version by Matumbi.

Mick plays a lazy lead guitar not dissimilar to a variation of the melody from 'Albatross' by Fleetwood Mac.

'Remote Control' – A knocked around full-on Rock version of the early classic with Mick's overdriven guitar turned up full. Maybe played and recorded to reclaim ownership of a great tune.

'Working And Waiting' – Instrumental run-through of a hard-rocking tune that would become (Working For The) 'Clampdown'.

'Heart & Mind' – Starting with a Buzzcocks-style guitar intro and then into a straight rock/pop tune with an offbeat Ska rhythm guitar, 'Heart & Mind' is a relatively lightweight song when compared to its peers on *London Calling*. The subject matter of the lyrics is the eternal human conflict between heart and head 'I've got heart, I've got mind / But I can't keep them in time'. The arrangement is adequate enough and Topper's drumming is quite reminiscent of his work on *The Cost Of Living EP*. In fact, this song was first alluded to in interview by Mick around the time of the Basing Street recordings in 1978. The overall impression is that 'Heart & Mind' was rightly considered by the band to be substandard for inclusion on either of the subsequent albums and in any case appears to have already been cannibalised by 'Groovy Times' in terms of musical content. The song is credited to 'The Clash' but ends with a coda incorporating a version of the old 101'ers song 'Keys To Your Heart'.

'Brand New Cadillac' – Light rockabilly work-through of the tune that was a 'warm-up' for the sessions.

'London Calling' – A slower tempo 'work-in-progress' version, indicating the relatively long gestation of what was to become a flagship song for The Clash. There were extensive sets of possible lyrics before the final version was decided upon. Joe can be heard still working out the words which took a lot of time and effort to finalise. His vocalised animal noises towards the end are much closer to the original idea of (riverside) seagulls than the canine-sounding calls on the final version.

'Revolution Rock' – In this, the pick of the bunch, The Clash sound right at home jamming the backing track. The technical quality of the recording is variable, but it's a good overall performance built on Topper's percussive skills. He would later comment that *London Calling* was the first Clash record where he felt that he could progress from being a 'Rock drummer' and begin to experiment with different percussion.

Selected Bootleg Recordings

'Rat Patrol From Fort Bragg' (Double LP) (1982)

The legendary 'lost' Clash album has appeared in different bootlegged guises over the years with various permutations/inclusions/exclusions of tracks. It has appeared under the title *Another Combat Rock* but is best known by the name *Rat Patrol From Fort Bragg*. At around 81 minutes long it sounds like an album that has not been finished. Mick Jones' was mainly responsible for the production, which sounds a little 'thin' and has a raw and unpolished quality. Described by Joe as Jonesy's 'home movie mix', it is rambling and unfocused but invites the listener on a sonic journey that takes some surprising detours. There are different arrangements, additional lyrics and (unedited) extended versions. (Many of these 'additional' lyrics actually appear printed on the inner sleeve of *Combat Rock*).

On the instructions of Bernie and Joe, the tapes were handed over to Glyn Johns for remixing and to edit the tracks down into a single LP. Johns encouraged the band to re-record several vocals and generally improved the production for the whole of the album that would become *Combat Rock*, but there is no doubt that *Rat Patrol* has a certain chaotic charm and is worth hearing. Various incarnations are circulating as bootlegs featuring remixes and instrumental versions, some of which could have been part of the aborted plan to include a set of 'dance mixes' on a bonus 12" single to be included with the LP. These alternative versions can be tracked down online by the sufficiently tenacious Clash fanatic. As recordings have circulated, the track listing for *Rat Patrol* has varied slightly, but the following content is more or less consistent.

1. 'The Beautiful People Are Ugly Too' (The Clash) Lead vocal – Mick

This tune (which has the alternative title 'The Fulham Connection') appears to have been a Topper Headon composition, perhaps with additional lyrics by either Mick or Joe, but has nevertheless been credited to 'The Clash'. The syncopated Afro/Caribbean backing track tune reappeared as the instrumental 'Casablanca' on Topper's solo *Leave It To Luck EP*, released in 1985. The calypso feel of the drums has echoes of 'Let's Go Crazy'. Lyrically, 'Beautiful People' appears to be confessional in that it looks at the illusions created by drug use 'There's gonna be a lot of washing when the dance is through'. The cheesy, lightweight feel of the instrumentation mirrors a sense of the vacuous superficiality of fame and celebrity. There is also a rueful glance towards the future where an old acquaintance is 'Stiffed out on the Itchycoo Park bench'. ('Itchycoo Park' was a classic 1960s psychedelic song recorded by The Small Faces with none other than Glyn Johns as their studio engineer).

2. 'Idle In Kangaroo Court' (The Clash) Lead vocal – Joe

An outtake from *Rat Patrol*, and sometimes given the alternative title of 'Kill Time'. A relatively weak and repetitive melody carries a lyric about workers selling their time to the rat race and subsequently being too busy to speak to other people that might stop them in the street. The snubbed narrator notes that 'You've sold your time but I've still got mine'. The steel drums and percussion drive the momentum, and lazy brass adds colour, but overall the song is substandard for The Clash and so was understandably not included on *Combat Rock*.

3. 'Should I Stay Or Should I Go' (Strummer/Jones) Lead vocal – Mick

The mix aside, Mick's original version of his best known song has a few differences from the one on *Combat Rock*. For example, in the second verse of the *Rat Patrol* version, the lead and backing vocals swap places in the running order. There is a cameo saxophone part in this version and Mick's vocal is either double tracked or treated with reverb and panned simultaneously left and right. These original vocal takes also have more of a trans-Atlantic twang and include the line 'Around the front or on your back'. This lyric was substituted in the final version (making it much more radio/TV friendly) with the consequence that it was much more likely to receive airplay and become a hit – which it did. Glyn Johns was no fool.

4. 'Rock The Casbah' (Strummer/Jones/Headon) Lead vocal – Joe

This version still has the original vocal take, but is essentially the same track as on *Combat Rock* albeit with a short percussive intro and a different, thinner sounding mix. Some versions of *Rat Patrol* include an additional extended remix version with the main vocal taken over by Ranking Roger from The Beat (aka 'The English Beat') who toasts over the backing track.

5. 'Know Your Rights' (Strummer/Jones) Lead vocal – Joe

This version features the original vocal which is mostly spoken and only partly sung and has more implied humour than the one re-recorded for *Combat Rock*, so in that sense it works better. The lyric meanders in and out of that of the final version and the whole track is just over five minutes long, compared to one that appeared on *Combat Rock* which is 3.40.

6. 'Red Angel Dragnet' (Strummer/Simonon) Lead vocal – Paul

This version is longer by a minute and a half than the one on *Combat Rock*, partly due to the inclusion of an additional 'verse' towards the end. This neither enhances nor diminishes the track because it is not a particularly good song and was a bit of a 'filler' in the first place.

7. 'Ghetto Defendant' (Strummer/Jones/Simonon) Lead vocal – Joe

This version was re-mastered by Mick and included on *Sound System*. It is around 90 seconds longer than the one on *Combat Rock*. Allen Ginsberg contributed to lyrics, particularly in the extra verse that poetically juxtaposes street level inequality with expensive nuclear weapons where 'Armies fight with suns'. This verse was edited out by Glyn Johns for the final version of *Combat Rock* and Ginsberg has never been credited as a co-author. Overall, Joe's vocal sounds less assertive and more lethargic than in the *Combat Rock* version. This *Rat Patrol* version is sluggish by comparison but is not without charm.

8. 'Sean Flynn' (The Clash) Lead vocal – Joe
This extended version includes more prominent instrumentation and therefore sounds a bit 'busy' and lacks the space and atmosphere of the *Combat Rock* version. This extended version also gives the impression that the arrangement has not been finalised, but the brutal culling of three minutes to bring it to a satisfactory length for inclusion on a single LP, smacks of the tail wagging the dog. The ambience of the Glyn Johns (*Combat Rock*) version is better, so it's a shame that he didn't get the option of producing the original full-length recording. This longer unedited version did eventually become officially available when it was remixed and re-mastered by Mick for inclusion on *Sound System*.

9. 'Car Jamming' (Strummer/Jones/Simonon) Lead vocal – Joe
This has a noisier and thinner sounding mix, with a longer outro but the content is not too different from the *Combat Rock* version.

10. 'Inoculated City' (Strummer/Jones) Lead vocal – Mick
This version is longer than the *Combat Rock* version at 4.27 compared to 2.42. It has an extended outro which includes samples of junk TV and advertisements randomly inserted into the backing track. (Mick was increasingly getting into using samples in this period and would take this further in his next band, Big Audio Dynamite). The 'Flushco' advert is at the end of the extended section of the track.

11. 'Death Is A Star' (Strummer/Jones) Lead vocal – Joe
This is the one song on *Rat Patrol* that is significantly shorter than the final Glyn Johns mix. This is mostly because the *Combat Rock* version has an additional instrumental intro/verse at 2.38.

12. 'Walk Evil Talk' (Headon)
This is an outtake recording of Topper enjoying himself playing double-time swing-feel drums. It's a lengthy instrumental with no significant melody other than the simple motif that is periodically repeated on the piano (also played by Topper). The track doesn't really go anywhere and could legitimately be pointed to as a good example of self-indulgence in the *Rat Patrol* sessions. It features prominently as background music in *The Rise And Fall Of The Clash* documentary.

13. 'Atom Tan' (Strummer/Jones) Lead vocal – Joe/Mick
Essentially the same content as the version on *Combat Rock* but with a slightly longer outro.

14. 'Overpowered By Funk' (Strummer/Jones/Headon) Lead vocal – Joe/Mick

Mick's early drafts of *Rat Patrol* didn't include 'Overpowered By Funk' at all. It was initially being kept apart for a separate purpose in the first instance, either as a 'stand-alone' release or to be included on a bonus 12" disc with the LP. This alternative method of release never materialised, however, traces of it can be detected in 'New York' mix of 'Overpowered By Funk' that is pretty close to the version that can be found on *Rat Patrol*. This excellent extended version of 'Overpowered By Funk' makes much more sense in this context as a 12" dance mix entity in itself rather than the edited down version that was grafted onto *Combat Rock* where it seems to sound slightly out of place.

15. 'First Night Back In London' (Strummer/Jones/Simonon) Lead vocal – Joe

Essentially identical to the B-side of the 'Know Your Rights' single.

16. 'Cool Confusion' (Strummer/Jones/Headon) Lead vocal – Joe

Although it was recorded in the *Rat Patrol* sessions, 'Cool Confusion' did not make it onto *Combat Rock*. It first surfaced 'officially' in the USA where it appeared on the B-side of 'Should I stay Or Should I Go'.

Disillusioned and disappointed with celebrity and fame and after getting swept up with the discarded bottles and detritus of stardom, the suggested solution is to '...send Cinderella's shoe back'. The melody is poor, but the arrangement is interesting. In common with most of the outtakes appearing on *Rat Patrol*, 'Cool Confusion' is a generally sub-standard song that is indicative of the diminishing output of the band at the time. An interesting curiosity, but not a classic.

17. 'Straight To Hell' (The Clash) Lead vocal – Joe

As it is with *Combat Rock*, 'Straight To Hell' is the real jewel in the crown of *Rat Patrol*. An additional minute and a half contains more lyrics, Strummer ad-libs and forays into his trademark 'Pidgin Spanish'. This version was remixed and re-mastered by Mick and included on *Sound System*.

'The Last Gang In Town' (rarities 1976-1984)

Also known as *Children Of The Revolution*, this collection was released in 2003 and comprises the following tracks – some of which have been officially released in the interim;

1. '1977' from *The Polydor Demos*.
2. 'White Riot' from *The Polydor Demos*.
3. 'Garageland' – Complete *Rude Boy* soundtrack outtake.
4. 'Pressure Drop' – Unreleased version recorded at the same session as 'Complete Control' and featuring Gary Barnacle on saxophone.
5. '(White Man) In Hammersmith Palais' – a re-worked alternative version recorded with Sandy Pearlman during the Basing Street sessions for *Give*

123

'em Enough Rope. It was donated to the 'Rock Against Racism' compilation LP.

6. 'All The Young Punks' – Demo version from the 4-track 'home' recordings made at Rehearsal Rehearsals in January 1978.

7. 'Safe European Home' – Live at The Music Machine, Camden Town 27 July 1978 recorded for the *Rude Boy* movie.

8. 'Lost In The Supermarket' – Live at The Majestic Theatre, San Antonio, Texas 22 May 1983.

9. 'Revolution Dub' – *Rude Boy* soundtrack version of 'Revolution Rock' recorded at Wessex without brass and keyboards.

10. 'Return To Brixton' – 1990 Jeremy Healy remix version of 'Guns Of Brixton'.

11. 'The Magnificent Seven (Dirty Harry mix)' – A remix of 'The Magnificent Dance' by the WBLS DJ Frankie Crocker that includes cinematic samples from the movie *Dirty Harry* as well as audio from Bugs Bunny cartoons.

12. 'Capital Air' – A one-off punk/poetry live experiment involving Allen Ginsberg performed live at Bond's, Times Square, New York City on 10 June 1981.

13. 'Should I Stay Or Should I Go' from *Rat Patrol From Fort Bragg*.

14. 'Walk Evil Talk' – A much shorter edit of the track from *Rat Patrol From Fort Bragg*.

15. 'This Is England' – 7" single version released in The Netherlands.

16. 'Career Opportunities' from *The Polydor Demos*.

17. 'Janie Jones' from *The Polydor Demos*.

18. 'London's Burning' from *The Polydor Demos*.

19. 'Tommy Gun' – Live from Dunfermline Kinema 6 July 1978. Recorded for the *Rude Boy* movie.

20. 'English Civil War' – Live from The Lyceum, London 3 January 1979. Although the sleeve notes confirm the date of this recording as being in January 1979, it is the same recording that appears on the *Sound System* box set dated 28 December 1978. It was recorded for *Rude Boy* but not used in the movie.

21. 'Outside Broadcast' from the 'Radio Clash' 12" EP.

22. 'The Beautiful People Are Ugly Too' from *Rat Patrol From Fort Bragg*.

23. 'Kill Time' from *Rat Patrol From Fort Bragg*.

The Clash On Broadway Disc 4 (The Outtakes)

This bootleg is packaged to appear like a legitimate release. It mainly contains remixes, minor studio outtakes and versions of *Cut The Crap* era material that are irrelevant. There are three outtakes from the *Sandinista!* Sessions: 'Louie Louie' and 'King Of The Road' (both covers) and one Mick Jones track 'Blonde Rock & Roll' which is pretty awful (the title gives it away, really) – a vacuous bubblegum song that doesn't even reach the low standards of something as poor as '1-2 Crush On You'. Also appearing is the version of 'Rock The Casbah' with Ranking Roger on vocals, toasting to the backing track, but it is not a particularly worthy rendition. This collection is for anally retentive completists only.

Selected Live Bootlegs

Joe was always reticent about releasing any live recordings while The Clash were together. The live footage showcased in *Rude Boy* had been overdubbed to improve it, and other recordings included on *From Here To Eternity* may well have been at least partly doctored in a similar fashion.

Pure bootleg recordings are by definition unembellished, 'warts and all' and lack proper production, but can contain electrifying performances. There are a large number of Clash bootlegs around that are of mixed quality and more are appearing all the time as live broadcasts are made available and put out for sale. My advice is to avoid these unless you've heard them prior to purchase. With all due respect to Terry Chimes and Pete Howard, anything recorded after Topper's exit in April 1982 is (in my view) a waste of time and money. What follows is a small selection of bootlegs recommended for the diehard Clash enthusiast.

Live at The Lyceum, London 3 January 1979

This is The Clash just after the release of *Give 'em Enough Rope* but before the release of 'English Civil War'. This concert was recorded properly on a 16-track for use in the *Rude Boy* film. It would appear that the six live recordings dated 28 December 1978 that appear on *Sound System* are actually from this concert, so they benefit from Mick's production and mastering for that collection. In any case, the additional inclusion of the other songs makes this is a relatively good bootleg recording of a really good performance.

Hammersmith Odeon 27 December 1979

Also titled *White Men In Hammersmith Odeon*, this good quality bootleg appears to have been recorded as one of the *Concerts For The People Of Kampuchea* organised by Paul McCartney (see note 18). The Clash agreed to play support to Ian Dury & The Blockheads for this very worthy cause, so it is a short set of only 16 songs. The performance also served as a 'warm-up' for the imminent '16 Tons Tour'.

Recorded hot on the heels of the release of *London Calling*, the songs from that album sound particularly fresh and energetic. Mickey Gallagher joins in from 'Jimmy Jazz' onwards, improving the overall texture of the music. Apart from 'Armagideon Time' (the only Clash song to make it into the movie and the associated LP), the other great performances include 'Jimmy Jazz', 'Wrong 'em Boyo' and 'Janie Jones'. Of particular interest is an early version of 'Bankrobber', played at a faster Ska tempo.

16 Tons Tour – 1980

Named with typical Clash gallows-humour after the financial mess the band were in ('another day older and deeper in debt...'), the '16 Tons Tour' showcases The Clash at their most musically cohesive. Mickey Gallagher was the unofficial 5th member of the band (as he had been for the 'Take The 5th Tour' of the USA the previous year). Unfortunately, there do not appear to be any good quality recordings of any entire performances, but tantalising glimpses have surfaced in various places. A performance recorded for television in Paris on 27 February was edited down to 13 songs including 'Protex Blue' and 'Koka Kola' and released on vinyl.

The only complete recordings that have appeared from the Lewisham Odeon concert on 18 February are of poor quality. Luckily, good quality recordings of individual songs from this concert have surfaced, the best of which is the magnificent performance of 'Capital Radio' that graces *From Here To Eternity* alongside 'Armagideon Time' which also features Mikey Dread. 'Clampdown' and 'Train In Vain' from that same concert were filmed by Don Letts and can be found on the DVD issued with the *London Calling – 25th Anniversary Edition*.

Live In Amsterdam 10 May 1981

Full of energy and recorded during the 'Impossible Mission Tour' at Jaap Edenhal in Amsterdam, this bootleg finds The Clash playing plenty of material from *Sandinista!* There is a fine performance of 'Charlie Don't Surf' wherein Joe drops in part of a monologue from the movie *Apocalypse Now*. 'Ivan Meets GI Joe' is notable for a rare lead vocal by Topper whose drumming still sounds sharp. Paul's playing gets a bit exposed on 'The Magnificent Seven', but overall a reasonably good bootleg of The Clash.

Bond's, New York City 28 May – 13 June 1981

There are several recordings from the 17 gigs at Bond's that were intended for radio broadcast and/or for use by Don Letts for his aborted *Clash On Broadway* film. The sets showcased plenty of material from *Sandinista!* including a great arrangement of 'The Call Up'. The versions of 'Train In Vain' and 'Complete Control' that appear on *From Here To Eternity* are from the concert on 13th June.

The Clash on Film and Video

Audio Ammunition (2013)
A brief, five-part journey through the five studio albums by The Clash giving a thumbnail sketch of each. A good, concise companion to the re-mastered five album box set.

The Future Is Unwritten (2007)
The warts and all Joe Strummer Story as told by his friend Julien Temple. This film was compiled after Joe's death and features contributions from the other Clash members Mick, Topper, Terry Chimes and Keith Levene (Paul is notably absent) as well as close friends and family. It covers his entire biography and is very well laid out to give an understanding of the man, his achievements, his demons and his eventful life. There is a stellar cast of witnesses and friends including Bono, Martin Scorsese, Matt Dillon and Johnny Depp as well as musical allies such as Tymon Dogg and Antony Genn. The film went on to win the Best British Documentary at the British Independent Film Awards in 2007. A very good film.

The Julien Temple Archive (2013)
Included in the DVD released with *Sound System* is a short collection of early Clash footage made by Julien Temple. There are some shots of The Clash singing 'I'm So Bored With The USA' in the Beaconsfield sessions as well as various scenes of the band milling around the streets in the vicinity of their permanent base of the time – 'Rehearsal Rehearsals' in Camden Town. There are also some scenes of the band at Mick's Gran's in Wilmcote House and some live footage. The Beaconsfield footage aside, there is no contemporary audio track with the film.

The Last Testament (2004)
A short film by Don Letts about the making of the *London Calling* album. It was released on a DVD and included in the 25th Anniversary edition of that album. There are interviews with the band, but also Kosmo Vinyl (PR man and general fixer) and Pennie Smith (Photographer). There are also some short sections taken from an interview with the unsung hero of this period of The Clash's history – the engineer Bill Price. In addition to the talking heads, the film includes short snippets of audio outtakes and some concurrent video footage in Wessex Studio.

(The Clash) MTV Rockumentary (1991)
A very brief introduction to The Clash timed to coincide with the release of *The Clash On Broadway*.

Rebel Truce (2007)
An hour-long decent telling of the tale of The Clash and the punk rock scene in 1970s London from which they emerged. Unfortunately Mick is the only

interviewee from the classic Clash line-up although there are interviews featuring Vince White (from the post-Mick Jones era) and Rob Harper (who was The Clash's drummer on the 'Anarchy' tour). Also interviewed are Don Letts, Tony James, Glen Matlock (of The Sex Pistols) and Steve Diggle (of The Buzzcocks).

The Rise And Fall Of The Clash (2014)

A film mostly about the break up of the band and the subsequent post-Mick Jones period aka 'The Pantomime Clash'. Ironically the only new interview from the classic line up is with Mick Jones. There are interviews with Terry Chimes and other witnesses, but the accounts of Pete Howard, Nick Sheppard and Vince White give the best insight into why the band was finished and Bernie Rhodes' hand in accelerating its destruction.

The film is mostly a look at the grimy underbelly of the end of The Clash and the music plays second fiddle to the uncomfortably honest narrative. It doesn't really celebrate The Clash's music at its best, but there are some snippets of rare rough recordings from the early days and some outtakes from *Rude Boy*. A more accurate title might have been 'The Fall Of The Clash' or 'Why *Cut The Crap* isn't a Clash album at all'. An interesting film for completists but not essential viewing.

Rude Boy (1980)

This movie was made by Jack Hazan and David Mingay and is a strange sort of precursor to the 'reality TV' genre. The film itself is generally shabby and doesn't have a 'plot' as such, but focuses on a fictional member of The Clash entourage – 'Ray' who is filmed at various gigs and studio settings. At two hours long, there is a lot of yobbish nonsense included and the underlying 'political' content is unfocussed and often sinks to the clumsy stereotypes of the era. The film as a cinematic piece is poor, but Clash fans will enjoy some of the 'behind the scenes' footage as well as the opportunity to see the band playing live. Unfortunately, almost all of the 'live' performances were actually overdubbed at Wessex and Air studios some time later.

On the positive side, the Rock Against Racism gig in Victoria Park, London on 30 April 1978 was filmed as part of the project, and there is other live footage including The Glasgow Apollo on 4 July 1978 when Joe and Paul were arrested after the show (although the scenes involving bouncers beating up fans were staged at a later date). There is also footage from May/June 1978 of The Clash in the studio recording the initial vocal takes for *Give 'em Enough Rope*. Towards the end of the film is a short scene where Joe plays a self-penned blues tune called 'I Ain't Got No Reason' followed by an old blues standard 'Let The Good Times Roll' while accompanying himself on the piano. Some of the 'live' tracks appear on the *From Here To Eternity* album – 'London's Burning', 'What's My Name' and 'I Fought The Law'. The film also features raw versions of 'Revolution Rock' and 'Rudie Can't Fail' recorded at Wessex to augment the soundtrack. The version of 'Rudie Can't Fail' over the final credits is taken from the *London Calling* LP.

The Clash had little to do with the general sweep of the film and were unhappy with the end product to the extent that they distanced themselves from it prior to its release. *Rude Boy* is worth watching for The Clash performances (albeit overdubbed) but not much else.

Viva Joe Strummer – The Clash And Beyond (2005)
Definitely worth watching, this hour-long account of Joe and his music features extensive contributions from his good friend, the articulate Tymon Dogg who allows us to hear one of the rare audio recordings from 1974 of Joe playing guitar to Woody Guthrie's 'I Ain't Got No Home'. The story is told of Joe's musical journey from his early days, via The 101'ers and The Clash to The Mescaleros with plenty of live footage. Some of the captions superimposed on the live footage are a bit suspect, for example describing 'Police And Thieves' as '...encouraging violent revolution'(?)

The film features an interview with Mick Jones who comes across as instantly likeable and friendly. There are also interviews with the disarmingly honest Topper Headon, Glen Matlock (The Sex Pistols), Pablo Cook (The Mescaleros) and various friends and associates including the roadie, Johnny Green. The live footage includes the unmissable occasion when Mick got onstage with Joe and the Mescaleros at Acton Town Hall on 15 November 2002 – just a few weeks before Joe's death.

Westway To The World (2000)
This is probably the best Rockumentary on The Clash by associate and sidekick Don Letts. Released in 2000 when Joe was still with us, Letts does a good job of providing a concise narrative of the band. He pieces together a wide range of live footage and other material to give a broad overview of who The Clash were and what they managed to achieve. All four members of the classic line up are interviewed as are Terry Chimes and Bill Price. Joe and Mick are particularly likeable as they reflect on their own failings in the story, but it is Topper (clearly still ill) who pulls at the heartstrings as he apologises for his part in the demise of the band.

The chronology of the images is much better than other Clash documentaries, but some of the captions are incorrect (for example, the gig in Victoria Park took place in 1978, not 1977). The film saves the blushes of the *Cut The Crap* era by ending at the sacking of Mick Jones in 1983. Joe put it this way; '1984 and we were gone, really. It was all over, bar the brushing out the room'. *Westway To The World* won a Grammy award and is highly recommended viewing.

White Riot Promo Film (1977)
Included in the DVD released with *Sound System*, this short promotional film shows the early Clash performing live versions of '1977', 'White Riot' and 'London's Burning'. This last track showed up on the B-side of 'Remote Control' single.

Best Live Concert Footage

A fair amount of live performances are available on the internet for viewing, but a large proportion of these postdate Topper's exit and are thus of dubious value. What follows is a small selection of recommended viewing.

Sussex University (1977)

There are four live songs filmed at Sussex University that are included in the DVD released with *Sound System*. They are 'I'm So Bored With The USA', 'Hate And War', 'Career Opportunities' and 'Remote Control'. It is poor quality black and white footage and the sound is also poor, but an interesting chance to see The Clash playing so early in their career.

Elizabethan Ballroom – Manchester (1977)

This is fantastic footage of an early Clash gig filmed on the 15 of November 1977 for the TV show, *So It Goes*. The four songs filmed were 'Capital Radio', 'Janie Jones', 'What's My Name' and 'Garageland'. The performance of 'What's My Name' is particularly good. Joe's antipathy towards television may or may not be an affectation, but the fact remains that at that time The Clash were generally absent from the airwaves, both radio and TV. The footage captures the early Clash at their sweaty, petulant best. It's interesting to note that there is not one Mohawk haircut in the house – a punk stereotype that actually postdates punk.

Music Machine – Camden, London (1978)

'Complete Control', 'Safe European Home' and 'What's My Name'. This footage is from the *Rude Boy* movie so is almost certainly overdubbed.

Lyceum – London (1979)

The definitive performance of 'I Fought The Law' as seen on *Rude Boy* and as heard on *The Clash On Broadway* and *Sound System*.

Lewisham Odeon, London (1980)

This footage shows The Clash on the '16 Tons' tour playing on home turf in South London. Mickey Gallagher can be seen playing the keyboards behind Mick Jones. Don Letts filmed the band playing 'Train In Vain' and 'Clampdown' – probably because they were at that time deemed the most likely songs to be released as singles from *London Calling* in territories outside the UK. This was the same concert where the magnificent performance of 'Capital Radio' was captured for the *From Here To Eternity* album. This is The Clash at the top of their game.

After The Clash

Joe Strummer

After the undignified end of The Clash, Joe went through a very difficult period. He deeply regretted the sacking of Mick and Topper and the fact that he had clearly put too much faith in the judgement of Bernie Rhodes. Any animosity between former band members was very short-lived. Joe tried to get Mick back into his band again, but by then Mick's new band BAD had already built up a head of steam, and so he declined the offer. Joe went on to co-produce BAD's second album and co-write five of the songs, but his solo career immediately thereafter consisted mainly of acting small bit-parts in movies and writing the associated soundtracks. He worked with The Pogues for a while, helping with recording and live performances, but this was as a favour, and clearly not where he saw his future. Joe was signed to Epic from his days with The Clash and he couldn't get out of the contract, releasing a single 'Trash City' and an album *Earthquake Weather* – both of which have some value but neither of which come anywhere close to his best work.

Joe was a complex character and friends saw him constantly beating himself up for (as he saw it) letting the best band in the world slip through his fingers. His work on movie soundtracks provided an income, but as an artist, he was floundering. Royalties from Clash recordings increased significantly with the release of retrospective compilations, but the posthumous profile of The Clash was raised most significantly in 1991 after the re-releases of 'Should I Stay Or Should I Go' and 'Rock The Casbah'.

Joe's 'wilderness years' continued until around 1994 – it was as if he was doing some sort of self-imposed penance in order to exorcise the ghost of The Clash. Then in 1995 he both re-married and also found a turning point at the Glastonbury festival. There he had a minor epiphany as he rediscovered his sense of a spiritual musical collective, this time around the campfires. The music sessions around these same campfires also rekindled his interest in World Music and a couple of years later, Joe secured a position with the BBC World Service broadcasting a weekly show to a global audience of around 40 million souls. Still gradually finding his feet, Joe got involved in a couple of novelty football records until eventually in 1997 Epic released him from his contract. This gave Joe a new lease of life and also gave him the opportunity to move in whatever musical direction he wanted to. This new possibility was also facilitated by the income stream resulting from the release of even more Clash retrospectives by CBS.

Joe the met former Pulp and Elastica member Antony Genn and began work on what would become the *Rock Art And The X-Ray Style* album. Joe assembled The Mescaleros and the band began gigging in June 1999 – one of the first gigs being at Glastonbury on 26 June. (A bootleg recording of the gig exists titled *Avalon By Bus*) [36]. *Rock Art And The X-Ray Style* was released on 18 October that year to critical acclaim. The high points include the magnificent 'Sandpaper Blues', followed by 'X-Ray Style', 'Yalla Yalla' and the wonderful, lilting, 3/4 time 'Willesden To Cricklewood'. This last track illustrated Joe's insight and ability to raise nondescript urban districts to semi-mythical status. On the next album, he transformed the status of the 'Ilminster bypass' from the mundane to the majestic.

Joe amicably parted company with Genn the following year and began work on his next album, *Global-A-Go-Go*. The writing and recording was well underway when, after a chance meeting in London with his old friend Tymon Dogg, Joe invited him to play on the album and eventually to join The Mescaleros.

If you only buy one album by Joe Strummer and The Mescaleros, make it *Global A-Go-Go*. With this album's release on 24 July 2001, Joe reached a pinnacle of creativity that ranks alongside his best work with The Clash. High points include 'Bhindi Bhagee' – a most articulate endorsement of the virtues of multicultural London. From food to music to community, Joe extols the absolute joy and vitality of cultural cross-fertilisation in an anthem of all that is great in the human family 'Welcome stranger to the humble neighbourhoods'. The title track of the album is a lyrical whistle-stop tour of World Music. 'Johnny Appleseed' is an ode to the working class ('If you're after getting the honey / Then you don't go killing all the bees'), and 'Shaktar Donetsk' (sic) is a big-hearted exercise in kindness and empathy for the desperate plight of refugees and illegal immigrants the likes of which has not been seen nor heard since the days of Woody Guthrie. *Global-A-Go-Go* is an absolutely remarkable achievement that illustrates the upward trajectory of Joe and his music at the time. He managed his renaissance whilst still staying under the radar of mainstream culture, just how he liked it.

Joe Strummer and The Mescaleros played a benefit gig for striking Firefighters on 15 November 2002 at Acton Town Hall. The recording of this concert is definitely worth tracking down if you can get a copy. It features songs from the first two Mescaleros albums, some (at that time) unreleased songs like the brilliant 'Get Down Moses', and a few Clash standards thrown in for good measure. It also happened to be a concert attended by Mick Jones, who on the spur of the moment jumped on stage during the encore and played three songs with Joe and the band [37]. This long overdue but spontaneous reunification of Joe and Mick was especially poignant because Joe died suddenly on the 22 December that same year. Joe's untimely death from a heart condition was tragic in the extreme for his wife, his children and his friends and family. It was also shocking to his fans and the wider world.

A posthumous album was lovingly produced, arranged and compiled by Martin Slattery and Scott Shields – painstakingly built up from unreleased recordings, demos and guide vocal tracks into a third and final album from Joe Strummer and the Mescaleros titled *Streetcore*. Alongside 'Get Down Moses' and a version of Bob Marley's 'Redemption Song' was another absolute tour de force in 'Ramshackle Day Parade'. The album finishes with a Fats Domino tune, 'Silver and Gold' and ends with Joe saying 'OK – That's a take!'

Joe Strummer 1952-2002. A one-off musician, an outstanding lyricist and an absolute legend. Rest in Peace, Joe.

Mick Jones

When Joe realised his own mistake in sacking Mick, he visited him and asked him to rejoin The Clash, but Mick already had other fish to fry and gracefully declined the offer. After the initial shock of being sacked from his own band, Mick had recovered quickly and formed Big Audio Dynamite (BAD) with Don Letts, Leo Williams, Dan Donovan and Greg Roberts. The debut album *This Is Big Audio Dynamite* was released in 1985.

The album contains three great songs 'Medicine Show', 'E=MC²' and 'The Bottom Line'. Musically, Mick skillfully blends his guitar work with more contemporary dance beats and samples (particularly cinematic ones). This is where the connection is most evident that links Mick's work on *Rat Patrol From Fort Bragg* to his new band. As further evidence of reconciliation with Joe, the second album *No 10, Upping Street* features some songs co-written by the two of them. Joe also helped to produce the album.

1988 saw the release of BAD's third album, *Tighten Up Vol. 88* (for which Paul designed the artwork), but that same year Mick had fallen seriously ill with pneumonia and spent some two weeks in a coma. BAD broke up the following year as Mick went through a period of recovery from his illness, but he formed a new band – 'BAD II' and was making music again very soon thereafter.

1991 saw Mick's profile rising when Levi Jeans asked if they could use The Clash's 'Should I Stay Or Should I Go' for an advert. The rest of the (former) band deferred to Mick as it was his song, and he allowed Levi's to go ahead. The song was re-released and became The Clash's biggest hit when it went to #1 in the UK. On the one hand, Mick's decision to allow Levi's to use the song can legitimately be construed as 'turning rebellion into money' – unthinkable to punk purists. On the other hand, it undoubtedly lifted The Clash into the public consciousness as never before, raising them from partial/relative obscurity into iconic status – and opening up their music to a new generation of fans. It was also understandable insofar as Mick's ambition had always been to enjoy a career in music '...and bunk the train to stardom...', and this was a sensible step to consolidate his long term future as a musician/producer. From 1991 on, the main four former members of The Clash enjoyed financial security as their back-catalogue continued to generate revenue, making opportunities possible that might never have otherwise presented themselves.

In 2002 and 2004 Mick produced The Libertines' first and second albums and he has been prolific throughout his career in his collaborations with other artists including Aztec Camera, Elvis Costello, Mick Ronson, Gorillaz and Primal Scream. He also formed 'Carbon/Silicon' with his old friend from the London SS days, Tony James.

Mick re-mastered The Clash back catalogue including hitherto rejected material from his unfinished opus *Rat Patrol From Fort Bragg* and oversaw the release of *Sound System* as a top-quality, 'once and for all' exhaustive compendium of The Clash.

Paul Simonon

Paul was the last man standing when The Clash finally gave up the ghost. He went straight back to his first love – painting – and this has remained his main occupation ever since. He has however been involved in several adventures – including some musical projects.

He played bass on Bob Dylan's *Down In The Groove*, released in 1988. Paul's involvement was peripheral, and it was a poor album, slated by the critics. That same year he designed the artwork for BAD's third album, *Tighten Up Vol. 88* for which his painting adorns the front cover. Paul started another band, 'Havana 3 am' which was occasionally active over the next few years, but his next 'release' was in 1990 when he commissioned Jeremy Healy to remix 'Guns Of Brixton' under the new title 'Return To Brixton' which reached #57 in the UK charts. Then in 1991 the long-awaited eponymous album *Havana 3 am* was released. This was the same year that The Clash profile was well and truly resurrected in mainstream consciousness by the successful re-release of 'Should I Stay Or Should I Go'. Then, characteristically his own man, Paul returned to painting again.

With The Clash's legacy becoming more widely appreciated, Paul again involved himself in the artwork for the live album *From Here To Eternity* in 1999. He later started a new musical initiative with Damon Albarn, 'The Good, The Bad & The Queen', and they released their debut album in 2007. In 2010 Paul played bass on the Gorillaz album *Plastic Beach* which also featured Mick Jones on guitar. In 2011 he spent two weeks in jail in Greenland after boarding an Arctic oil rig with other Greenpeace activists. 2013 saw the release of *Sound System* with its exquisite packaging (verging on the opulent) – again designed by Paul. Then in 2018, he released another album with 'The Good, The Bad & The Queen' titled *Merrie Land*.

The Clash were offered huge sums of money to reform and Paul was put under pressure to do so, but he always held the line and declined. Joe's death in 2002 put an end to any further speculation around a reunion concert. Paul may have been the least musically gifted member of The Clash, but he sure as hell knew what The Clash stood for. He stood his ground and saw it through to the end.

Nicky 'Topper' Headon

Topper loved being in The Clash, but from the high point of *London Calling* on, his alcoholism and addiction to hard drugs dragged him down into the abyss. After getting busted for possession of heroin at Heathrow Airport in 1981, various lifelines had been thrown to him, but he didn't take any. His sacking from The Clash in 1982 accelerated his desperate downwards spiral, although in the early days he could still function sufficiently to release some records including his solo album *Waking Up* in 1985. Then in 1987 Topper sank to an absolute low when he was convicted of supplying heroin to another user, Barry Waller who subsequently died. Topper spent 15 months in jail, but on his release, he immediately reverted to his old ways and at one point was badly injured in a car crash. He had contracted hepatitis, was destitute and had reputedly sold his Clash gold discs to fund his habit. Whilst being interviewed by Don Letts for the *Westway To The World* documentary (2000), Topper apologised to the other members of the band for 'letting the side down', but he looks ill in the footage which indicates that he was still using at that time.

Joe's untimely death in 2002 shook Topper who believed that due to his own actions, he deserved to die long before Joe. Two years later Topper was clean. He rediscovered his love of drumming with local musicians and started 'Narcotics Anonymous' in his current home town of Dover. He now spends his time doing charity work and playing the drums for the pure joy of it.

Buying The Clash's music

Because the Clash's music was spread over several 'stand-alone' singles and EPs as well as the five studio albums (disregarding the non-Clash album *Cut The Crap*) it can be hard to know where to start with them, so here are my suggestions;

Firstly, simply work your way through the albums *The Clash, Give 'em Enough Rope, London Calling, Sandinista!* and *Combat Rock* chronologically (preferably on vinyl) and do not waste your money on *Cut The Crap*. The five studio albums are also available as a re-mastered CD box set (see above).

If you still want more (and there is plenty more), then you could try *The Singles* album which should fill in a lot of the spaces in between. Alternatively, *The Singles Box Set* will make your collection even better because it contains all the B-sides too (and they are definitely worth having – although most of these are on *Super Black Market Clash*).

If you are a non-obsessive completist and have already forked out on the above, then you could do worse than topping up with *Black Market Clash* for the sake of 'Robber Dub' and 'Time Is Tight'. For absolute obsessives, there is also the *Sound System* CD box set which is a bit pricy but does contain almost every studio recording. If streaming or downloading The Clash's music, *Sound System* is the most comprehensive collection.

Regarding live recordings, there are various bootlegs around, but official releases include *From Here To Eternity* which contains some great recordings (see above). *Live at Shea Stadium* is the band going through the motions without Topper in 1982 and is not recommended.

If you can get hold of a copy, The 7" vinyl *Cost Of Living EP* is also worth acquiring because of the often overlooked '5th track' which is unnamed and un-indexed but is known as the 'Cost of Living Advert' or alternatively 'I Fought The Law (reprise)'.

In short;

If you want a one-album introduction to The Clash, then buy *The Singles* album.

If you want the best introduction to The Clash, then buy the five studio albums.

Once you have paid out for the above, you can fill in most of the gaps by buying *Super Black Market Clash*.

This really only leaves you short of 'Armagideon Time' and the original version of 'Capital Radio' – both of which are on *Black Market Clash*. The best live album is *From Here To Eternity*.

After acquiring all of the above, it's a matter for Clash connoisseurs and obsessives only. The (CD format) *Sound System* collection is excellent and almost comprehensive but is expensive as a one-off purchase.

Recommended Books

The Last Gang in Town – Marcus Gray

Redemption Song – Chris Salewicz

Notes

(1) The overall sweep of the narrative constitutes my understanding of events. My first exposure to The Clash was in a stairwell of a council estate in South London where a fellow-teenager showed me his 'White Riot' 7" single that he had just bought. Two things that struck me were how short the songs were, and the fact that the title of the song on the B-side was '1977' – the current year. It occurred to me then that this music was very much of the moment. I was 14 years old, so not quite in a position to go to gigs just yet, but I did get every Clash record as soon as it came out from thereon – and I was hooked. I bought into the excitement and possibilities opened up by punk and new wave music. There was no internet. You couldn't see The Clash on TV or hear them on the radio – if you wanted to hear them then you had to seek them out. The first time I saw them play live was in February 1980 at The Lewisham Odeon (when the live version of 'Capital Radio' was recorded) with Mikey Dread supporting. They were brilliant. I made sure that I saw them every time they played in London on tour from thereon. I was also lucky enough to see Joe Strummer playing with The Mescaleros just before the release of the album *Global-A-Go-Go* (which is, incidentally highly recommended). The Clash had a profound effect on me and on the life choices I made. The individual members may well have had feet of clay, but collectively – as The Clash – they remain one of the best rock and roll bands of all time. I hope this book helps the reader to share in the enjoyment and appreciation of 'The only band that matters'.

(2) By 1985, punk reached its logical conclusion as Bob Geldof (of The Boomtown Rats) really did change the world with Live Aid – saving countless people from starvation and calling the Ethiopian dictator Mengistu a 'cunt' to his face.

(3) Bernie Rhodes was the manager of The Clash from the start and was crucial in their approach from the beginning. There would have been no Clash without Bernie Rhodes. It was Bernie that introduced Mick and Paul to Joe, and it was Bernie that encouraged them to write songs about issues that were relevant to them for the first album. He was very influential in the early punk movement and famously refused to allow the embryonic Siouxsie and The Banshees to use The Clash's amps because of their swastikas. He encouraged The Clash to nail their anti-fascist colours to the mast from the off – when it was not necessarily fashionable to do so. Bernie worked with Paul on the artwork for the records and was an absolutely intrinsic part of creating the whole concept of The Clash. The band had a complex relationship with Rhodes who became increasingly overbearing, distracted and on occasion just plain absent at crucial times when he was most needed. Mick and Bernie had a particularly difficult relationship as time went on, and Rhodes parted company with the band just after *Give 'em Enough Rope* was recorded.

After a short, chaotic period of 'self-management', the band was taken on by Blackhill Management (who were also looking after Ian Dury &

The Blockheads) with Kosmo Vinyl assisting. This move ran alongside the band's most creatively glorious but financially unsustainable period, recording and releasing *London Calling* and *Sandinista!* The lack of a commercial rudder went hand in hand with arguably their best two albums and the cementing of their legacy.

Rhodes returned to manage The Clash after *Sandinista!* He brought in Glyn Johns as producer to edit down *Combat Rock* and in doing so made the album more accessible than the original sprawling effort, provisionally titled *Rat Patrol From Fort Bragg*. Rhodes encouraged Joe to sack Topper, citing the latter's heroin addiction as the reason – which is fair enough; although Topper claimed that none of his performances were affected by his addiction. Mick was becoming increasingly unhappy with Rhodes' interference in the creative process of the music and the chasm began to widen with Mick on one side and Bernie, Joe and Paul on the other. The band had clearly run its course but was paradoxically enjoying commercial success for the first time. This financial upturn masked the fact that The Clash had reached their collective expiry date and this manifested itself in the injudicious sacking of Mick.

Rhodes appears to have believed that he owned The Clash 'brand' and subsequently displayed another astonishing lack of judgement with his part in the recording and release of *Cut The Crap*. So he is both hero and villain. The Clash wouldn't have happened without him, but he shamelessly had his fingers in the pie and tarnished The Clash's hitherto unblemished musical legacy with a disastrously shite sixth album.

(4)   After *Combat Rock*, Joe wrote a song – 'House Of The Ju-Ju Queen' for Janie Jones. She recorded it at Wessex Studios in December 1982 with Joe, Mick, Paul and Mickey Gallagher and Charlie Charles (of the Blockheads) as her backing band under the nom de plume 'The Lash'. It's not a very good song, but it is a laugh.

(5)   The 'Garage' rock/bands referred to were part of an ongoing movement in New York at that time that included Television, Patti Smith and The Ramones. New York 'Garage' was a midwife to punk and the embryonic London scene of 1976 drew much influence from there.

(6)   The Clash played with the 'Year-Zero' concept in terms of wiping the slate clean so that new music could happen. The roots of the term actually related to the murderous 'Khmer Rouge' regime in Cambodia that had decided that any form of culture or education that predated the revolution was irrelevant and should be eliminated. This, in turn, led to atrocities and genocide (see note 18). The Clash clearly and unequivocally condemned such politics, but they had toyed with the 'Year Zero' concept in the incomparably more sedate context of music.

(7)   Although production was credited to Lee 'Scratch' Perry, the band later disclosed that Mick remixed the record with louder guitars after Perry had left the studio. Perry was a Jamaican reggae producer who happened to be in London recording with Bob Marley and the Wailers. He assisted Marley with 'Punky Reggae Party' in which the latter pays tribute to the 'new

wave' of punk bands coming through at the time;

The Wailers will be there / The Damned, The Jam, The Clash....

'Punky Reggae Party' appeared as the B-side of Marley's 'Jamming' from the (highly recommended) *Exodus* album.

(8)   Peter Green was a founder member of Fleetwood Mac. A very talented blues songwriter and guitarist, he fell foul of hallucinogenic drugs in 1970 when in, the words of bassist John McVie 'He did acid – all it took was a couple of tabs – and he never came back'.

(9)   Rock Against Racism (RAR) was a British political and cultural movement in the mid-1970s, set up to counter the rise of the far-right political groups and the associated street violence towards ethnic minorities. (For a more comprehensive introduction to RAR, try watching the movie *White Riot* by Rubika Shah). In 1980 The Clash donated an unreleased version of '(White Man) In Hammersmith Palais' to the compilation album *RAR's Greatest Hits*.

(10)   When the first tape of the demos intended for Guy Stevens was lost, Mick simply ran off another copy from the TEAC 4-track master. All copies of these original recordings were thought to have been lost but they re-surfaced much later when Mick found them in a box in his loft when he was moving house in 2004. A selection of the tracks was included in the 25th anniversary release of *London Calling* that same year under the name *The Vanilla Tapes*.

(11)   In 1979 the 'Cold War' was in full swing and a nuclear exchange between the Soviet Union and the USA bringing about 'mutually assured destruction' of the protagonists (and the entire human race) was a distinct possibility. London was in the firing line along with the rest of Europe.

(12)   Recreational drug use is, and has probably always been particularly ubiquitous in various music 'scenes' – a fact towards which wider society often displays an ambivalent attitude. Although a frequent smoker of weed himself, Joe was adamant when he opposed the use of hard drugs in general and opiates in particular. As with alcohol in previous generations, Strummer saw the temporary respite offered to the disenfranchised by getting wasted as a distraction and a diversion from getting to the real root of injustice in the world (see 'Ghetto Defendant'). There is, of course a huge element of hypocrisy going on here, especially considering the drug habits of certain members of the band. Strummer attempted to articulate his frustrations but never quite addressed these inconsistencies and contradictions.

(13)   The Spanish Civil War broke out in 1936 after years of political chaos when the democratically elected Republican government was challenged by a Nationalist military invasion led by the fascist General Franco. The USSR supported the Republican cause but undermined unity in the pursuit of Communist domination of the coalition. Germany's Nazi regime assisted Franco and this intervention was widely seen as Hitler

flexing his military muscles in a precursor to the impending World War. Franco's fascists were eventually victorious and he remained in power until his death in 1975.

The Spanish Civil War was notable for the number of anti-fascist volunteers from around the world that fought for the Republic in the 'International Brigades'. For an introduction to the International Brigades in The Spanish Civil War, try watching the movie *Land and Freedom* by Ken Loach.

(14) Joe was a huge fan of Federico Lorca, the Spanish poet and playwright who was murdered by the Fascists in the course of the civil war. At his lowest point, during the death-rattle of The Clash, Joe made an emotional pilgrimage to the vicinity of Lorca's grave (the exact location is unknown).

(15) The local authority's confused partial evacuation in the immediate aftermath resulted in an increase of public mistrust (Bruce Springsteen eloquently covered this subject matter in his song 'Roulette', recorded that same year).

(16) Named after the 'lost' river Effra that runs under Brixton.

(17) Simonon's somewhat unhealthy obsession with firearms aside (see 'Guns on the Roof'), the lyric does point to a 'front line' mentality that was certainly apparent in Brixton in the late 1970s. Heavy-handed police practices (including misuse of the 'Sus' laws), in tandem with overt or unconscious racism, had driven a clear dividing line between the police in Brixton and the large Jamaican community that resided there. This undercurrent of resentment against the abuse of power was accentuated by the recent election of the Thatcher government whose right-wing policies resulted in an economic recession that hit immigrant communities particularly hard. Meanwhile, tabloid papers spewed out racist stereotypes leading to a further sense of alienation.

Distrust of police, exacerbated by the frequently injudicious and disproportionate use of police powers had now made conflict inevitable and in April 1981 the Brixton Riots brought this festering inequality into the spotlight. 'Guns of Brixton' is – in a way – the companion piece to 'White Riot', but was more prophetic in as much as it was released some 16 months before the Brixton Riots took place.

'God save the Queen' by The Sex Pistols had reached #1 in the UK in jubilee week in 1977, and in another of those seminal moments when popular music perfectly encapsulated the zeitgeist, The Specials' 'Ghost Town' reached #1 in the UK charts in 1981. Meanwhile, The Clash found themselves being criticised for being away in America while Brixton burned. They pointed out that although they had predicted the riots, that it wouldn't have made any difference if they were there or not. Mick – who was from that part of London – was anyway unimpressed, failing to see the point of people burning down their own neighbourhood.

The 'Sus' laws were abolished that same year and the Brixton riots became a watershed moment for UK politics when a subsequent investigation by Lord Scarman contributed to the content of The Police and Criminal Evidence Act in 1984. This new legislation encouraged a move away from racist stereotyping by police and made them much more accountable for the exercising of their powers of arrest and/or 'Stop and Search'.

(18) Kampuchea was the name given to Cambodia in 1976 by the ultra-Maoist dictatorship, The Khmer Rouge. Their horrific, all too real 'year-zero' doctrine resulted in appalling human rights abuses including torture and mass genocide, wiping out some 25 per cent of the population. This despicable regime was ousted by the Vietnamese invasion of 1979 when the true scale of the human suffering became apparent to the outside world. Paul McCartney organised some *Concerts for the People of Kampuchea* to raise funds for the survivors and these happened to take place shortly after the release of *London Calling*. The Clash shared the bill with Ian Dury & The Blockheads on 27 December 1979 (see *White Men In Hammersmith Odeon* in the 'bootlegs' section). Other artists that performed in the associated series of concerts included Queen, The Who and McCartney himself. The performances were filmed and a compilation album was released which featured The Clash playing 'Armagideon Time'.

(19) Although the artwork from *Sandinista!* onwards mostly credits original songwriting authorship to 'The Clash' (i.e. Strummer/Jones/Simonon/ Headon), the songs were registered with the music publisher with more precise details naming the actual songwriters as agreed by the band. It is from these publishing records that I have allocated songwriting credits from *Sandinista!* onwards.

(20) The red and black colour scheme for the album mirrored the colours of the Sandinista Liberation Front (FSLN) flag. This was a socialist party in Nicaragua that had ousted the hated fascists of the Somoza regime and was improving the welfare of poor people through health, housing and education programmes. Literacy rates soared, but counter-revolutionaries (Contras) funded by the US government continuously attacked civilians and infrastructure in a general attempt to undermine the revolution (see 'Washington Bullets'). The fact that The Clash named their album as they did, helped to shine a spotlight on US foreign policy in Nicaragua. The Catalogue number for the original *Sandinista!* LP is 'FSLN1'.

(21) 'The Profumo Affair' was a British political sex-scandal involving the high-ranking government minister John Profumo unwittingly sharing his teenage mistress with a suspected Soviet spy. Profumo lied to parliament about the affair in 1963 and was eventually forced to resign. The subsequent inquiry by Lord Denning revealed associated perverse sexual practices by other members of the elite including one gentleman who had attended sex parties whilst donning a leather face mask. Given Joe's distain for the hypocrisy of those in power, he would have no doubt enjoyed this hilarious, salacious detail which he included in 'The Leader'.

Joe inherited a healthy scepticism of the elite from his father who – incidentally – knew the spy Kim Philby socially from his days at the Foreign Office.

(22) The general feeling of young men in the West Indian community was that they were being treated unfairly by the police under the 'Sus' laws due to racial prejudice (see note 17).

(23) With 'Police On My Back' on the B-side.

(24) Agent Orange is a toxic chemical defoliant that was used by the US military during the Vietnam War to destroy vegetation for tactical reasons. This resulted in an environmental catastrophe and a human tragedy that caused long-term health damage to both the indigenous population and also to US military personnel.

(25) Joe's love affair with Spanish dates back to his childhood years in Mexico City. In addition, some of the members of The 101'ers were in London while in exile from Pinochet's Chile and Joe's girlfriend at the time of The Clash's first album was the Spanish-born Poloma Romero (also known as 'Palmolive' – The drummer of punk band 'The Slits'). The Spanish language appears in different incarnations in several of his compositions (e.g. 'Spanish Bombs'), but most notably in 'Should I Stay Or Should I Go'. In this case, it adds spice to Mick's fourth and final love song for The Clash.

(26) The Guardian Angels were originally set up in New York in 1979 as a citizen-based group that carry out 'safety patrols' to deter criminality and to provide reassurance to the public. They are all volunteers and the organisation is non-profit making.

(27) Joe's lyrics frequently referenced the cinema (e.g. 'The Right Profile', 'Death Is A Star', 'Ramshackle Day Parade') and so it came as no surprise when The Clash struck up a friendship with both Scorsese and De Niro while they were in New York. Both men were fans of the band's music and had seen them play at Bond's in 1981. That same year, Mick and Joe were given roles as 'extras' in one scene of *The King Of Comedy* movie by Scorsese.

(28) This last death-rattle of Empire had the effect of diverting attention from inequality at home and boosting the sagging popularity of the very administration that had been one of the root causes of the hostilities in the first place.

(29) Possibly at least partly in answer to the strange 'Disco Sucks' phenomena in the USA at that time, where rock music fans set fire to disco records – conjuring up images of the fascistic fondness for book-burning (and bringing to mind the prophetic words of Heinrich Heine 'Where they burn books, in the end they will also burn human beings'). The Clash tried to introduce their fans to different varieties of music and (for example) invited The Sugarhill Gang to support them at the Bond's concerts in 1981. These bands often received a mixed reception from the fans.

(30) The 'Boat People' were Vietnamese refugees from the war and its aftermath.

(31) The Clash hooked up with Futura 2000 as one of the bright lights on the New York rappers/graffiti artists' scene. He toured with the band in 1981.

(32) Allen Ginsberg was one of the generation of American Beat Poets involved in the 1960s counter-culture. He can be seen in the background in the video of Dylan's 'Subterranean Homesick Blues' and had toured with him on the *Rolling Thunder Revue*.

(33) 'Should I Stay Or Should I Go' was released three times in The US in 1982. Firstly on 10 June, then on 24 June, and then on 20 July. The B-sides were 'Inoculated City', 'Cool Confusion' and 'First Night Back In London'.

(34) Unlike other big rock acts that had preceded punk, The Who never seemed to attract the scorn of the new movement like most of their contemporaries. This may be because their early songs like 'My Generation' and 'Substitute' are proto-punk songs themselves, sharing the common ancestor of defiant but imaginative working class realism, firmly rooted in the British perspective. Pete Townshend was particularly gracious towards musicians involved in punk and new wave, and at one point paid for Topper to get into a drugs rehab programme. Roger Daltrey later provided backing vocals on the title track of Strummer's *Global-A-Go-Go*.

(35) 'Vince' White's first name was actually 'Greg', but it was decreed that this was not 'punk' enough so he was duly re-christened with a more 'appropriate' name.

(36) *Avalon By Bus* is a bootleg recording of Joe Strummer and The Mescaleros playing at Glastonbury on 26 June 1999. It was his first and last performance at the festival he had grown to love so well. The new Mescaleros material is well performed, but Joe is audibly still in the process of getting his bearings in his latest musical incarnation. Consequently, the performances of the Clash material are unpolished as Joe searches for the most appropriate arrangements (although 'Straight To Hell' and 'Rock The Casbah' are clearly heading in the right direction). The title is a reference to the live album *Babylon By Bus* by Bob Marley and The Wailers. Joe enjoyed the ancient Arthurian myths that surrounded Glastonbury and the mystical qualities of Avalon so eloquently expressed in William Blake's *Jerusalem*. It's a typical Strummer prank to cross-fertilise Blake and Marley so poetically.

(37) Mick came onstage and completely surprised Joe during 'Bankrobber'. It was totally unplanned and spontaneous. They played 'White Riot' which was a very nice touch, because back in the days of The Clash, Mick was always trying to drop it from the setlist. They finished with 'London's Burning'.

The Clash had been offered huge sums of money to reform and never did. It's somehow fitting that Mick and Joe's reunion was for no money at all at a benefit gig for striking Firefighters. Joe's coffin was escorted by a guard of honour of Firemen at his funeral.

Would you like to write for Sonicbond Publishing?

We are mainly a music publisher, but we also occasionally publish in other genres including film and television. At Sonicbond Publishing we are always on the look-out for authors, particularly for our two main series.

On Track. Mixing fact with in depth analysis, the On Track series examines the entire recorded work of a particular musical artist or group. All genres are considered from easy listening and jazz to 60s soul to 90s pop, via rock and metal.

Decades. This series singles out a particular decade in an artist or group's history and focuses on that decade in more detail than may be allowed in the On Track series.

While professional writing experience would, of course, be an advantage, the most important qualification is to have real enthusiasm and knowledge of your subject. First-time authors are welcomed, but the ability to write well in English is essential.

Sonicbond Publishing has distribution throughout Europe and North America, and all our books are also published in E-book form. Authors will be paid a royalty based on sales of their book. Further details about our books are available from www.sonicbondpublishing.com. To contact us, complete the contact form there or email info@sonicbondpublishing.co.uk